# A FRESH HERB PLATTER

# A FRESH HERB PLATTER

DOROTHY CHILDS HOGNER

*Illustrated by Nils Hogner*

DOUBLEDAY & COMPANY, INC.
GARDEN CITY, NEW YORK
1961

*The jacket design is based on a culinary herb chart, published by the Herb Society of America.*

Library of Congress Catalog Card Number 61–8890

Printed in the United States of America
First Edition

A FRESH HERB PLATTER

for the epicurean who loves both
the good earth and good food

"Nor do I think Men will ever reach the End,
and far extended Limits of the Vegetable Kingdom . . ."

JOHN EVELYN,
—*Acetaria, A Discourse of Sallets,*
*London, 1699*

# CONTENTS



Items within the text printed in **bold face** may be located by consulting the Index.

# INTRODUCTION

Some gardeners remind us of an enthusiastic fisherman we know who loses all interest in a fish once he has reeled it in. Like our friend the fisherman, who is lured by the sport of fishing but gives his catch away, these gardeners look upon a garden only through horticultural eyes. Most of them are strictly flower lovers, but some use the same amount of muscle power and enthusiasm in raising vegetables for show. They delight in exhibiting at the county fair and winning a dollar and a blue ribbon for the finest squash. They raise excellent quality vegetables and trust the preparation of them for the table to someone else. To us, this is sacrilege.

In our case the gardener—or rather, the gardeners—are the cooks, for we both like to raise beautiful bumper vegetables and aromatic herbs and to create with them in the kitchen. We use a hoe, with one eye on the kitchen range.

Our favorite market is Crutch Frozen Food Locker Company, where we store our frozen herbs, vegetables, meats, and fish, and where, in addition to good service, we get the latest information about frozen foods from the "locker boys," Bob Peterson and Jim Fitzgerald. We wish to take this opportunity to thank them for many helpful suggestions.

We are particularly indebted to Raymond P. Atherton, agricultural economist and technical adviser on crops and soils for The Hubbard-Hall Chemical Company, for advice on soil chemistry.

# A FRESH HERB PLATTER

# 1. A VEGETABLE AND HERB GARDEN

One bitter cold January weekend, in the winter which we have dubbed the "Winter of the Deep Freeze" (1958–59), we arrived at our herb farm in the Berkshire Hills and found our water faucets in the house frozen. This had never happened before. Outside, the wind was howling, sixty miles an hour. The steep lane which leads to our place was a better skating rink than a road, and the gardens, the herb gardens, lay bare and brown and wretched, exposed to the drying winds; for the "poor man's manure," that savior of perennials wintering in the field in a cold climate, snow, had failed us. Again and again the weather bureau had forecast a substantial accumulation, but only a soupçon of snowflakes had fallen, and these the constant wind speedily swept away, leaving the gardens without the white blanket normal to our location.

The cold hung on; the frost bit deep, deep. Rumor had it that the local power-and-light company, making repairs on the main street of our home town, had found the ground frozen to a depth of five feet, eight inches, whereas plumbers installing water pipes in the Berkshire Hills plan only on a three-foot maximum depth. We did finally, in March, have two real snowstorms, too late.

As we waited with the green thumber's impatience for the

first signs of spring, we worried over our hardy perennial herbs. After the ground first froze, we had, it is true, mulched. As you shall see, we are addicts of mulching, but even with artificial cover, could the herbs stand such arctic-like treatment? The appearance of the mountain laurel (*Kalmia latifolia*) which grows luxuriantly around the herb gardens was alarming. The usually evergreen leaves looked as though someone had applied a blowtorch to them. Most of this hardy, wild native shrub appeared at least half dead of winter burn, so how could domestic herbs survive?

It seemed as if even the little peeper frogs, those natural forecasters who let us know when to expect the frozen ground to turn to mud, had gone into an eternal sleep. Finally their shrill voices sounded from the fire pool. Some at least had come through the bitter cold with enough strength to wriggle up out of their Stygian beds into the sunlight, but the sleigh-bell chorus was smaller than usual, and not nearly so enthusiastic.

And so it was, when at last the air rejoiced to the sounds of peeps and croakings, and Mr. Robin perched on the top of the tallest hemlock tree, singing for his mate, that we sloshed down the long rows of perennial herbs in the lower garden, expecting trouble; and we found what we expected. The loss of plant life was distressing.

There was not a sign of life in the peppermint bed. Of the spearmint which we call the Beach Day–Wagstaff mint, because the original plants had come via two friends' gardens to us, five weak plants showed up. A couple of handfuls of sturdy Scotch spearmint seedlings also showed, and some of the pretty *Mentha longifolia* and an unidentified hybrid. The pots of apple mint set in a cold frame came through alive. The apple mint in the field had died. All the lemon balm was gone, and all the garden thyme.

As spring advanced, each day we walked down to the bank covered with that rather insignificant little plant with the high-sounding botanical name, *Anthemis nobilis*—in plain English, camomile (medicinal tea, and blond hair rinse). Each day we got down on our knees and unbelievingly touched the brown leaves. They were dry; they crumbled. One-hundred-per-cent kill.

On the credit side of the ledger, our fine strain of tarragon came through in vigorous shape; so did the origanum and the carpeting thyme, and even that fussy grower, woolly carpeting thyme (*Thymus Serpyllum lanuginosus*), and costmary, of course—also catnip and sage.

By this time reports were coming in from other nurseries and from friends with gardens. There was nothing but dismay and astonishment in the exclamations heard.

We hasten to add that it is very doubtful if anyone in our area reading this book will again experience this kind of disaster. We shall have other troubles: too little or too much rain, and similar obstacles gardeners must hurdle, but experts agree that we shall not see another such winter as that of the Deep Freeze for the next half century.

So, with our morale boosted by this thought, we tackled our model family-size herb garden, in which had formerly grown a selected variety of culinary herbs, rescued what plants seemed strong and worthy and replanted the space, trying an entirely new look.

We set out to design a garden and ended by designing two. You choose which one you want to plant. The first is a combination vegetable-and-herb garden, but before getting out the stakes and guidelines, we pause long enough to inquire——

## WHAT IS A VEGETABLE?

This may appear to be a silly question. Everyone knows that a vegetable is a plant cultivated for food—a carrot, a beet, a turnip; and a more seemly question for this book would be: What is an herb?

However, a study of the old herbals brings to light the revealing fact that in former times the Old World vegetables, as well as the sweet or flavor herbs, were classed as herbs. Thus a carrot was as respectable an herb as dill or tarragon. Plants commonly cooked were called potherbs. And in this old herbal era, one took not only the essentially medicinal herbs, but also the vegetable herbs, such as onions, as a treatment to cure aches and pains; for the whole vegetable kingdom was then looked upon more or less as a medicine chest.

For example, as late as the time as the great seventeenth-century "sallet" maker, John Evelyn, a plain boiled onion was said to improve the appetite, "corroborate" the stomach, cut "phlegm," and "profit the asthmatical."

So much for old herbal lore. This is a book for the modern gardener and cook in which a vegetable is a vegetable, and a culinary herb is one of those sweet plants, the leaves or seeds—sometimes roots—of which improve the flavor of a dish. We leave it for the modern M.D.s to prove or disprove their healing worth.

We simply wanted to make the point that vegetables and the sweet, aromatic herbs had a close affinity for each other during the long history of Old World gardening; they belong together in a modern garden too, so that the cook-gardener can gather at hand's reach both the fresh vegetables and the fresh herbs he will use in the kitchen. Just as a fresh-picked, sun-warmed tomato exudes a full, rich fragrance, soon dissipated on the supermarket's shelf, so, too, a sprig of tarragon or other culinary herb freshly snipped from the plant has an incomparable savor.

## THE WHIRLING SQUARE

Enter the Vegetable and Herb Garden on the little brick path which leads to the circular bed of mint, and look about you. You are within a square, 25 by 25 feet. A square in itself is a dull shape, to be sure, but the square is merely the frame. We have revolted against planting vegetables in monotonous straight lines; we have laid out the rows to please the eye. The design is strictly ours. We do not pretend to have invented the scheme—that is, the idea of planting in a pattern (nothing new under the sun). We have in mind the pattern gardens popular in medieval times. It was then stylish to make knot gardens. Herbs were planted and pruned to give the effect of green and gray knotted ropes, intertwined; the result was fascinating, but of course this particular herb pattern is achieved only with certain special plants, such as the medicinal herbs, *Teucrium* and the *Santolinas,* which lend themselves to clipping. Obviously vegetables do not belong in this form. But vegetables, with a foil of herbs, can make as decorative a garden as one devoted solely to herbs. And so we let loose with a "Whirling Square." The garden plan is marked off around the edge, each mark indicating 1 foot, so that you can figure the length of the rows.

The core is the circular bed of mint, edged with bricks, 4 feet in diameter, inside measurement. Total bricks: 32. Bind the mint circle inside the bricks with a "fence" made of the common metal lawn edging carried by garden-supply stores. It should be at least 5 inches wide, and it should be sunk into the ground, leaving ½–1 inch above the surface, to prevent the mint from becoming an escapee.

Garnish the mint bed with a semicircle of shallots; next, a larger, three-quarter-circle of carrots, bordered by a quarter-circle of six tarragon plants, three plants on each side of the short row of Swiss chard.

In the next, ever-widening circle, plant kohlrabi, French sorrel, frying and bell peppers, flanked by a quarter-circle of dill, cut on one side by a reverse quarter-circle of okra. The matching twin row on the other side: fennel. The basil goes into two straight rows, bordering the little brick path. In the foreground, the semicircles are, to the left and right of the path: sweet marjoram and parsley, backed by a semicircle of coriander and sum-

30
31
31
32
29
28
27
26
10
12
11
7
6
5
8
3
9
33
4
4
2
21
34
1
19
35
16
18
20
17
25
13
13
14
15
22
N
22
23
24
36
W
E
S
37
38
SCALE
0'
1'
2'
3'
4'
5'

mer savory; then diagonally left, top onions and beets, and diagonally right, rocambole and rutabaga.

Now walk around the border of the 25-by-25-foot square. Beginning with the path, go east from a rosemary plant, past two sweet cicely and two lemon balm. Turn north, past a sage plant, two winter savory, and four garden thyme, skirted by a curved row of snap beans—and then two clumps of chives and a row of chervil planted in the shade of the long straight row of pole tomato plants. Coming back, start at the tall single lovage on the northwest corner, pass by the curved line of pole Limas, then by four red cabbage, two hyssop, and back toward the little brick path again, passing one pineapple sage and the second plant of rosemary.

To the south of the main garden, and on the other side of the cross path, we have laid out a bed 25 by 5 feet in which to plant space robbers we have chosen to include—namely, a 25-foot row of special peas and five hills of squash. Since these peas are an early, cold-weather crop, they will be past bearing and the vines can be removed before the squash have begun to spread.

The effect? Beautiful, this blend, this potpourri of annual and perennial sweet herbs, of dill and rosemary interplanted with curved rows of beets, beans, and other vegetables. But how about maintenance of the fancy curves? This is easy. We have kept maintenance uppermost in mind, but maintenance follows only

---

THE VEGETABLE AND HERB GARDEN

| | | | |
|---|---|---|---|
| 1 spearmint | 11 okra | 21 rutabaga | 31 tomatoes |
| 2 shallots | 12 fennel | 22 rosemary | 32 lovage |
| 3 carrots | 13 basil | 23 sweet cicely | 33 pole Limas |
| 4 tarragon | 14 sweet marjoram | 24 lemon balm | 34 red cabbage |
| 5 Swiss chard | 15 parsley | 25 sage | 35 hyssop |
| 6 kohlrabi | 16 coriander | 26 winter savory | 36 pineapple sage |
| 7 French sorrel | 17 summer savory | 27 garden thyme | 37 peas |
| 8 frying peppers | 18 top onions | 28 snap beans | 38 squash |
| 9 bell peppers | 19 beets | 29 chives | |
| 10 dill | 20 rocambole | 30 chervil | |

after preparation of the garden soil and planting. (First comes the ordering of the seeds and plants from seedsmen and plant growers, of course.)

We have given the common names of the plants in the garden designs—thus, carrots, thyme, etc. There follows a specific listing, noting the varieties of vegetables recommended and the botanical names of the herbs. Because someone may want to make a smaller garden, we have listed the plants in order of our preference for use in the kitchen.

## VEGETABLE PLANTS TO BUY

Unless you have a greenhouse or a cold frame in which to start your own tender seedlings, it is advisable to buy the following plants from a commercial grower.

**Tomatoes: 12 plants—4 big red, 2 orange, 3 plum, and 3 pear.**

There are certain old stand-by varieties which we raise year after year, but we usually try at least one new variety, if not of tomatoes, then of some other vegetable, each year; for how can anyone know whether the new hybrids are superior to the standard unless one tries them? It is also fun to experiment with an entirely new vegetable, even, and get out of the rut of beets, beans, and carrots.

In the Vegetable and Herb Garden there are two early- and two main-crop, big red tomatoes. For the first crop, we like the early standard Valiant, and also Burpee's Big Early Hybrid. Marglobe is hard to beat for the main crop. Jubilee is the name of the big orange variety. With regard to our choice of small tomatoes—the Red Plum and the Yellow Pear—so far as we know, there is only one variety of each.

We grow all of our tomatoes staked.

**Peppers: 12 plants—6 bell and 6 Italian sweet.**

The common peppers sold at the supermarket are bell peppers, the kind of peppers to stuff. These peppers are also good, of course, cut in strips or chopped, but our favorite general-use cooking pepper is the Italian sweet, Italianelle, sometimes sold under the name "frying peppers." They are long and rather narrow in shape, light green in color, and very mild and sweet in flavor.

**Cabbage, red:** 4 plants.

There is not room for many of the cabbage family in a garden of the size of our Vegetable and Herb Garden. Rather than the white or savoy, we prefer to raise the gourmet's cabbage, the red, a must in making borsch, the Russian national soup.

**VEGETABLE SEEDS TO BUY:** 1 packet each.

**Snap Beans**

We can never make up our minds whether we like the green or yellow wax snap beans better. So we alternate, and one year raise the green, and the next year the yellow wax. We did try raising both the same year, but, somewhat like the old woman who lived in a shoe, we had so many beans, we did not know what to do.

This year we are in the yellow cycle, and the variety is Surecrop Stringless Wax, also called Yellow, or Golden, Bountiful. The seed catalogue, which we always believe when trying a new variety, claimed Yellow Bountiful was uniformly stringless, and so it proved to be.

For the green-snap-bean year, we nominate Burpee's Tender Pod.

**Carrots**

We have tried many varieties of carrots, and always come back to the old standard, Danvers Half Long, which can be counted on to produce nice plump roots. It has a good flavor too.

**Beets**

Burpee's Extra Early, or the old standard, Crosby's Egyptian, also early, are equally good. A second sowing of Crosby's Egyptian will produce a fall crop, and it is a good winter keeper. Of course the harvest must be stored in a cool part of the cellar, partitioned off from the furnace room.

**Lima Beans**

We prefer pole to bush Limas because they are cleaner. One packet is enough to plant the ten poles, for which space is allowed in the Vegetable and Herb Garden. Burpee's Big 6 brings good results.

**Kohlrabi**

This refined member of the cabbage family is neglected by many home gardeners. The bulb, the part eaten, forms on the stem above the ground and has a good, rather mild flavor. It is an excellent vegetable, cooked, and may also be sliced and served raw in salads. One word of caution: Always pick kohlrabi young. As it matures, it gets tough and stringy, and soon becomes inedible. We prefer Early White Vienna to the purple variety.

**Swiss Chard**

Swiss chard is a kind of beet, propagated for leaves instead of roots. This is our choice for "spinach" greens. We are strict with ourselves. We limit our greens for the pot to one kind. Since we also have a variety of salad greens, we have almost a plethora as it is. A great advantage of chard over true spinach is that you can pull off and use the outer leaves, and if you do not damage the heart, new leaves will come all summer long. Lucullus is a good variety.

**Okra**

Clemson Spineless is a good variety.

**Rutabaga**

One either likes turnips or not. We do, especially the yellow Swede or rutabaga. We like to raise at least enough to serve at the holiday feasts, Thanksgiving and Christmas.

Burpee's Purple-Top Yellow is a good winter keeper.

## IN THE SQUASH BED

**Mange-Tout Peas:** 2 packets.

We have planted the straight row in the squash bed, over the path from the Vegetable and Herb Garden, with those delectable morsels, the *mange-tout* or edible podded peas. The young pods, picked when they have grown to their full length, but before the little seeds inside have swollen, are tender and delicious. The water in which they are cooked makes an excellent, savory vegetable-soup stock. A good variety is the Mammoth Melting Sugar.

Edible podded peas grow 3–4 feet tall and must have support.

**Squash:** 4 packets.

We have, over the years, raised so many different kinds of squash, we have run the gamut. We have boiled down the list to two varieties of summer and two of winter, planted in a total of five hills. We have long since given up the practice of hilling squash. We plant them, like other vegetables, on the level, for hills dry out. But, out of habit, "hilling" remains in our vocabulary.

The best and, in our opinion, irreplaceable squash, is Early Golden Summer Crookneck, two hills. There is nothing to beat this good old summer squash. You can have the newer Early Prolific Straightneck, which may yield more per squash. It is easier for the market grower to package, but has an inferior flavor and texture.

Our second choice: Fordhook zucchini, one hill. You can do lots with a zucchini which you cannot do with a crookneck. Zucchini is good sliced and sautéed, also baked; and baby zucchini, when sliced raw, makes the basis for a good canapé.

For the winter squash: one hill of acorn, variety, Table Queen, and one hill of Butternut. Both have long, trailing vines. The fruits are relatively small, and good winter keepers. We have discarded the old standard, Burpee's True Hubbard only because the fruit is too big for a family of two. The old Hubbard, with the help of plant scientists, did make a fashionable effort to reduce. The result, the Baby Blue Hubbard, is small, but it requires a great deal of space to trail, and under our care it has not produced well.

**Rosemary** (*Rosmarinus officinalis*): 2 plants.

Rosemary is so good with beef, fish, pork, and whatnot. This evergreen herb will grow up to 4 feet in height, but few nurseries sell plants of this big size. A plant 12 inches high will need about 1 square foot of garden space.

Rosemary is not winter hardy and must be potted and taken indoors, or put in a cold frame, in cold climates when frost threatens.

**Garden Thyme** (*Thymus vulgaris*): 4 plants.

We never, never make a fish or clam chowder without using thyme. Its common use in stews, etc., is too well known to need repeating. Thyme is usually winter hardy.

**Mint:** 4 plants.

Some people use any old mint, even horse mint (wild) in the kitchen. The mint we have selected for the Vegetable and Herb Garden is the gourmet's *Mentha spicata,* spearmint. Because spearmint is a popular flavor in chewing gum, some people do not realize that this is the best mint for both julep and lamb sauce.

In an average year, in a climate such as ours, where the temperature frequently reaches zero, spearmint can be counted on to come through in the garden in good condition.

Mint grows to a height of over 2 feet. The horizontal stems, called stolons, reach out and bury themselves in the soil, then sprout roots underground and come up to form new plants a few inches from the mother plant. This is the way mint travels, all over the place, unless confined, as already suggested.

## PERENNIAL HERB PLANTS* TO BUY

Many of the herbs for which we say "buy plants" may al raised from seeds, but it takes the seedlings so long to rea usable size that little harvest may be made of the leaves, at until the end of the first summer. Thyme takes forever to get enough to use. Rosemary takes longer than forever, or so it se to the eager cook. So unless you are blessed with a greenhou we urge starting the following perennial herbs from nurs plants.

Number One on our list is:

***Tarragon, Estragon** (*Artemisia Dracunculus*): 6 plants.

This delectable culinary herb was in ancient time treasured as one of the dragon herbs (*Dracunculus*), those herbs which were then believed to have the power to cure the bites of mad dogs and wild beasts. In our time, tarragon is a must with chicken recipes, a savory herb with fish, and a vinegar herb of note.

You have no choice but to buy plants, for the true gourmet's tarragon (*A. Dracunculus*) rarely sets viable seeds. When a seed house lists tarragon seed, and some do, you may be sure that it is not the gourmet's tarragon, but very likely the annual Russian tarragon, which is *nyet* delicate in flavor.

The true tarragon, a hardy herbaceous perennial, grows about 2 feet high, if allowed to mature. The cook keeps snipping and new sprouts come. Each plant requires 1 square foot of garden space.

Second on our list of herbs for which we suggest that you buy plants (we are listing them, like the vegetables, in order of our preference for use in the kitchen) is:

* Herbs with an asterisk came through the Winter of the Deep Freeze in excellent condition.

***Lovage** (*Levisticum officinale*): 1 plant.

We could scarcely make soup without lovage. It is a tall, rank grower, and reaches a height of over 6 feet. It is a very hardy herbaceous perennial.

**Winter Savory** (*Satureia montana*): 2 plants.

We like the flavor of the winter savory as much as we do the summer savory. The savories are traditional with string beans, and are "savory" fish herbs.

Winter savory grows about a foot high. It is fairly hardy, but it is safer to pot and winter plants in a cold frame in New England.

***Sweet Cicely** (*Myrrhis odorata*): 2 plants.

Sweet cicely, also called giant sweet chervil, is a very decorative plant with graceful, fernlike leaves and pretty white flowers. It grows up to 3 feet high. The leaves, the root, and the hard seeds (each about ⅞ of an inch long) have a strong anise flavor.

**Lemon Balm** (*Melissa officinalis*): 2 plants.

Lemon balm is usually winter hardy. It is about 2 feet tall at maturity. The leaves are good with any recipe that calls for lemon flavor. Lemon verbena (*Lippia citriodora*), the better known scented lemon-leaf herb, is nipped by the first frost.

***Sage** (*Salvia officinalis*): 1 plant.

Near the tail end of our list of perennial herbs to be raised from plants comes sage, which is as familiar to Americans as parsley. We use it in few recipes, other than at holiday time. One plant will give more leaves than you will need for the stuffing of the traditional holiday bird, turkey. Even if you make your own sausage, or sage cheese, there will probably be enough leaves for your needs on 1 plant, for sage is a very strong herb, and a little goes a long way.

**Pineapple Sage** (*Salvia rutilans*): 1 plant.

Quite new to most gardeners, this handsome cousin of garden sage grows up to 3 feet in height. The luscious leaves have a pleasant pineapple fragrance and taste. The flowers are scarlet. It is a very tender subshrub and must be brought into the house when frost threatens.

***Carpeting Thyme** (*Thymus Serpyllum*): 25 plants.

For a pretty effect, plant carpeting thyme between the bricks in the paths. This is the low, creeping thyme. There are many varieties, among them the beautiful little crimson-flowered *Thymus Serpyllum coccineus* and the gray-leafed woolly thyme (*T. Serpyllum lanuginosus*). Both of these, however, are slow spreaders, and if you wish to fill the cracks between the bricks quickly, buy the common mother-of-thyme (*T. Serpyllum*), which has pale mauve flowers. It spreads fast.

Mother-of-thyme may be used in the kitchen, but the taller-growing garden thyme is preferred because of its size.

***Hyssop** (*Hyssopus officinalis*): 2 plants.

This is not the hyssop spoken of in the Bible as springing from a wall. The culinary hyssop is a shrubby plant that grows over 2 feet tall and makes a good hedging plant, resembling in growth a dwarf box. The leaves are rather dominant in flavor. We use them occasionally in stews and similar dishes.

## THE LILY FAMILY

Now we come to the lily family, for which you buy bulbs. The culinary lilies are, of course, onions (genus *Allium*). This genus contains an amazing variety of plants. Some, such as molly, which has pretty yellow flowers, are raised in herb gardens for their decorative value.

Among our favorite common onions are the big sweet Spanish or Bermuda onions, and the big Italian red onions, but we do not raise them. A good quality of these, and also of the small white onions most often served creamed, are easily found in the market. We prefer to give space in the Vegetable and Herb Garden to more unusual onions that few grocers stock.

***Shallots** (*Allium ascalonicum*): 36 bulbs.

These small onions, which in French are called *échalotes,* are very choice and have a special, sweet flavor of their own. Added to the roasting pan with beef, or chopped to use for stuffing, or with a sauce, they rate number one among onions. The pinkish-white color of the inner skin is characteristic. So too are the cloves, for the bulb of a shallot is not whole, like that of a common onion, but formed like garlic, of cloves. Sometimes there may be only two cloves to one bulb, other times five or six.

Three dozen bulbs will bring an increase, when planted, of up to a hundred bulbs, depending upon the number of cloves in each bulb. You separate the shallots and plant the cloves, and not the whole bulbs. They will winter over in the garden but do best if they are taken up in the fall and replanted in the spring.

***Garlic** (*Allium sativum*)

We cannot cook without garlic, but we do not raise the common kind (*A. sativum*). We used to, and if you try, plant in extremely rich soil. But most markets carry good-quality common garlic, and garlic raised in the home garden is no better, so why bother? Besides, there is an interesting kind of garlic which you cannot buy in any market we have been in, and this we do raise. This garlic is commonly called:

***Rocambole** (*Allium Scorodoprasum*): 12 bulbs.

Rocambole is also called giant garlic, not because of the size of the bulbs, but because of the height of the flowering stalks. It may be substituted in any recipe calling for common garlic. The flavor is milder.

The bulb that grows in the ground is whole, and not divided into cloves, like market garlic. It has a fascinating way of growing and of propagation. The top of the flowering stalk bears a white bulb with a pointed tip that reminds one of the head of a long-billed bird. Inside the mother bulb is a cluster of tiny aerial bulbs, called bulblets, which grow and cause the mother bulb to swell, and finally the jacket bursts.

By now the weight of the mass of bulblets is too much for the stalk to bear; it bends to the ground, or the bulblets drop off and thus replant themselves.

***Top or Egyptian Onion** (*Allium Cepa viviparum*): 4 bulbs.

As the name *viviparum,* live bearing, indicates, this is

another self-planter. The top onion is a much bigger plant than "giant garlic," the stems and leaves are thicker and much taller, and the aerial bulbs which the flowering stalk produces are also bigger than the bulblets of rocambole. Out of the bulblets come contorted green tongues. Occasionally one of these bulblets will bear more aerial bulbs at the end of its tongue. Inevitably this weighty increase becomes too heavy for the flowering stalk, and it bends and sets the bulblets on the ground.

The top onion is useful because the mature bulbs which winter over in the ground may be eaten in early spring. The hollow leaves, harvested when young and tender, may be filled with a canapé mix.

***Chives** (*Allium Schœnoprasum*): 2 clumps.

We would never plant any kind of vegetable or herb garden without chives. These little bunching onions, whose leaves have such a delicate flavor, are a must. How could we make meat balls without them? Well, one can chop plain onions as a substitute, but they are not the same. By all means, chives—two big clumps. Chives are so well known, it is perhaps unnecessary to explain that a bunch is composed of dozens of narrow wee bulbs, each of which sends up tasty leaves for the cook to snip. Cut them back and they will come again and again and spread.

**HERB SEEDS TO BUY:** 1 packet each.

**Basil** (*Ocimum Basilicum*), rhymes with "dazzle."

Basil is the herb that goes hand in hand with tomatoes. There are several species of basil. Purple basil is very decorative, and so is the curly-leaf basil. Both are edible, but sweet basil (*O. Basilicum*), which grows to a height of about 18 inches, and has large light green leaves, is the number-one culinary choice. Basil is a tender annual and should be planted after danger of frost is past.

**Dill** (*Anethum graveolens*)

Dill, of dill-pickle fame, has an affinity for shellfish. When boiling shrimp, always add several sprigs of fresh dill. The essential oil in dill helps to neutralize the strong shellfishy odor during cooking and adds a piquant flavor to the shrimp.

We generally sow dill at the same time as basil, but it may be sown as soon as the ground may be worked, for it self-sows in our New England climate.

## WHAT IS MARJORAM?

This is a question frequently asked by visitors at our herb farm, and with good reason. The considerable confusion over the identification of marjoram stems from the simple fact that there are several *different* species of herbs, all commonly called marjoram. The leaves of these different marjorams have a similar though not identical flavor, and one may be substituted for another in the same recipe.

The matter of the botanical classification has been hashed over by herb growers and written up in horticultural magazines. Finally clarified, it boils down to this.

The three species of marjoram most often offered by herb nurseries in this country are: wild marjoram (*Origanum vulgare*), pot marjoram (*Majorana onites*), and sweet marjoram, until recently classified botanically as *Origanum majorana*.

The first of these, *O. vulgare,* grows wild in the United States. The leaves are almost tasteless, and this plant should not be allowed in the culinary garden or, more especially, in the kitchen. The nurseryman, however, may stock the imported English wild marjoram, which is often listed in catalogues simply as "origanum." This English wild marjoram has aromatic leaves. Incidentally, it rates an asterisk for hardiness.

The second marjoram mentioned, pot marjoram, *M. onites,* is not winter hardy. *Onites* is very likely a source of the dried herb commonly carried in Italian grocery stores under the name "orégano."

The last-mentioned marjoram, *O. majorana,* is the most important to the cook. It has recently been reclassified and has been officially crowned the horticultural marjoram, *Majorana hortensis*. This is the true marjoram offered by seed houses, under the name "sweet marjoram."

**Sweet Marjoram** (*Majorana hortensis*)

Sweet marjoram has the best flavor of all the origanum-marjoram-oréganos. Buy it with confidence. It is a perennial, but those who live in cold climates must treat it as an annual, for it is not winter hardy. It is very easily raised from seed.

Sweet marjoram is a natural ingredient for meat balls, meat loaf, and spaghetti sauce. A few leaves, chopped fine, add a savory flavor to herb butter for broiled steak.

**Summer Savory** (*Satureia hortensis*)

This is the annual counterpart of winter savory, a tender annual which should be sown after danger of frost is past. It grows up to 18 inches in height.

**Chervil** (*Anthriscus cerefolium*)

A light green cousin of parsley, chervil may be sown as soon as the ground may be worked in the spring. It has a special affinity for eggs and is a necessity for a French herb omelet.

Like parsley, it is a biennial, flowering the second year. Early in the spring of the second year a few leaves may be garnered, but it soon bolts and is best treated as an annual.

**Fennel or Finocchio** (*Fœniculum dulce*)

Also called Florence fennel. Fennel is a dual-purpose culinary herb. It is a sweet herb, and is also cooked as a vegetable. The leaves, chopped fine, are excellent with fish and the bulbous oval base is a tasty potherb, especially good served with a fish menu.

***French Sorrel** (*Rumex scutatus*)

This is the sorrel with which the French make the notable sorrel soup. The leaves look similar to the leaves of its cousin, wild dock and, like dock, it is a rank grower. The raw leaves can be used in salads, but sparingly, for they are quite sour and acid in taste.

Cut the flower stems as soon as they come. If allowed to set seed, the plants often die out.

**Coriander** (*Coriandrum sativum*)

The fruit (seeds) of coriander resemble peppercorns. They are one of the ingredients used in making curry. The seeds germinate well. Coriander is easy to raise and not given to disease or bugginess, perhaps because of the extreme, shall we say "fragrance" of the leaves? On a hot, humid day, they literally stink. Because of this, we never thought of using any part of coriander, except the seeds, in the kitchen. One day, however, we were telephoned by a friend who wanted to know if we would like to have some Chinese parsley. Thinking that this was an herb new to us, we drove over to her place. Her Chinese parsley turned out to be coriander, which incidentally does have a leaf that reminds one of flat-leafed, true parsley. Our friend informed us that the leaves of "Chinese parsley" are used by the Chinese in salads.

We tried it. We shall stick with the common parsley, thank you, for to our palates, as much as we like the seeds, the leaves of coriander taste just like they smell.

Some years later someone else asked us about a Puerto Rican soup recipe that called for three leaves of *culantro,* or Spanish parsley. What was it? We immediately suspected that it was our friend coriander again. We searched Spanish dictionaries, without success. Then, happening to meet a friend who is a fluent Spanish linguist, we asked her, "What is *culantro?"*

"Coriander, of course," she replied. "But you are not pronouncing it correctly. It is c*i**lantro.*"

We have since learned that coriander leaves are also popular for use in salads in South America and Egypt.

All this has done for us is to bolster our growing suspicion that common plant names can lead one down all sorts of strange culinary alleys. We shall, of course, try Spanish parsley soup as soon as our coriander is in full leaf.

Speaking of parsley at such length, we come at last to:

**Parsley** (*Petroselinum hortense*)

We have left the true, the horticultural parsley, to the last, not because we like it the least. We use oodles of it. But it is planted by everyone who makes a vegetable garden; its leaves have been used for their good flavor and as a universal garnish, even during that period when herbs went out of fashion in America. Most people plant it, or buy it at a supermarket, or at any rate they get it somehow, somewhere, and use it, without ever thinking of it as an herb.

We had an amusing experience in this connection. A Turkish diplomat happened to come to our place and we showed him an herb chart we had designed, featuring a selection of popular culinary herbs. Because most common culinary herbs are native to the Mediterranean region, he was quite familiar with them. But after he had studied the chart closely he said, "You have left out the most common herb."

We thought of hyssop and various other exotic herbs, which might seem common to a Turk, but which we had not included in this elementary chart. To each one he said, "No, no." He added, "I mean the one you see sold in every supermarket in America."

We took a second look at our chart, and there it was, not featured in the main chart itself, but in the lower border—it was the garnish for the design, and it was, of course, parsley.

You can plant this revered biennial herb as early as the ground can be worked. Like chervil, the leaves may be gathered the second spring, but it soon flowers; the leaves become tough; and it is best treated as an annual.

The variety of parsley you plant is a personal choice. We prefer the moss-curled because it has a good flavor, it chops more easily than the plain or flat-leafed, and it is a very decorative garnish. You may also use the leaves of the parsnip-rooted or Hamburg parsley which is raised principally as a root vegetable.

## WHERE CAN YOU BUY HERB PLANTS AND SEEDS?

Ten years ago, this was a problem. But as the renaissance in herbs jets ahead, it is becoming ever easier to locate a source. First, try your local nursery and your favorite seedsmen. Many general nurseries are stocking a limited selection of popular herb plants in the most demand, such as tarragon and rosemary. The big seed houses such as Harris, Burpee, Breck, Max Schling, and Comstock, Ferre & Co., to mention a few, carry at least the common kinds of herb seeds, including dill, sweet marjoram, and summer savory. You can even buy a surprising variety at the little seed stands that sprout in grocery stores and drugstores in the springtime.

The Herb Society of America, Horticultural Hall, 300 Massachusetts Avenue, Boston 15, Massachusetts, publishes *The Herb Buyer's Guide* (10 cents), giving sources of herb plants, seeds, and products.

Once the plants and seeds are ordered, the gardener must check to make certain that the soil is in an hospitable mood to receive them. Then come the questions of how deep to plant, how thick to sow, and how to set plants in the garden, all of which are answered in Chapter 3. General directions apply alike to preparing, planting, and maintaining the Vegetable and Herb Garden, the Garden Salad Bowl and Annex.

## 2. A GARDEN SALAD BOWL

This is a salad bowl into which the salad maker walks and, standing on the central path, reaches out and picks the mixings, crisp lettuce, fragrant leafy herbs, corn salad, upland cress, tomatoes, sleek cucumbers and what-have-you. The result is even more satisfying than one might imagine.

The design for the salad garden is an oval bowl, 18 feet long and 13 feet wide, outlined with bricks set on end. Down the center runs a path—3 bricks wide; 136 bricks to make the length—which is interrupted, off center, at the location of the compass by a flagstone, 2 by 2 feet, to break the monotony of the bricks.

The flagstone is flanked by two cucumber hills. The cucumbers are trained on twin 8-foot, white-painted wooden trellises, the kind easily obtainable at garden-supply shops. We "climb" our cucumbers, to save space, to make a decorative effect in the garden, and, not least, to permit the fruit to grow in perfect form, unmarked by contact with the soil.

At the north end of the garden is a 2-foot-square mint bed, edged with boards, each sunk at least 4 inches into the ground, to keep the mint from running out of bounds.

Starting one curve to the right, and one to the left, of the mint bed (see diagram), are three Yellow Pear and three Red Plum tomato plants, tied to sturdy stakes. Continue along the outside rim of the Salad Bowl. After the tomatoes come the peppers, four plants on either side. The peppers end on the east border at a clump of costmary, and on the west, at a beautiful fernlike plant of sweet cicely. Two feet square are allowed for this plant and for the costmary, which should, like mint, be confined with boards or a metal strip.

Keep following the outside rim, and you will come next to the twin 6-foot beds of basil, one on each side, then to a 6-foot bed of tarragon, balanced by a 6-foot bed of upland cress. Now, at the southern border, two 2×2 foot stands of borage guard the path. Walk north on the path; the pattern of the garden branches out in a candelabra of greens. The first branch, inside the outer row to the east, is planted with scallions, which end at the costmary. To the west, Chinese cabbage ends at the plant of sweet cicely. Continue past the second row above the sweet cicely and the costmary; remark the twin rows of dill.

Turn your back on the mint. A plant of lemon balm burgeons on either side of the path. Beyond, in the third inner circle, are two short rows of rocket, right and left, and finally some lettuce. Start down the west side past escarole; on the east side is endive; then a row of parsley extending clear back to the path. On the opposite side is Ruby lettuce. Turn around and face north again. There are six clumps of chives, three on each side, and on the left, a row of frying peppers; then cos lettuce goes back to the path. On the east is a row of Oakleaf, then Imperial lettuce, and back to the chives.

Start again in ever-narrowing rings, with two arms. South of the cucumbers are two rows of bibb lettuce, and north are two rows of radishes, one white, one red. Directly edging the path are corn salad and salad burnet.

4
3
2
15
15
5
14
16
16
14
5
7
6
28
27
29
29
23
24
N
W
E
S
1
1
8
8
17
18
30
30
26
26
22
25
21
21
19
20
13
12
9
10
11
11
SCALE
0
1'
2'
3'
4'
5

In the design of the Garden Salad Bowl, we have given the common names of the sweet herbs, the vegetables, and the lettuce. When more than one variety of a specific kind of lettuce is offered by seedsmen, we so indicate in the following listing.

**Head Lettuce:** buy seeds, 1 packet each.

One of the old, standard-size, and most reliable of the head lettuces for the home gardener is Imperial No. 44. It can usually be depended upon to head, even during warm weather. Imperial No. 847 has larger heads and is almost as heat-resistant as Imperial No. 44.

Bibb is the midget, spring-weather, gourmet's lettuce, with small, tender heads.

Cos or romaine, sold under the varietal name of Paris White and Parris Island, grows with an upright, not a round head, reaching about 10 inches in height. It is usually dependable, even during warm weather.

---

THE GARDEN SALAD BOWL

| | | | | | |
|---|---|---|---|---|---|
| 1 | cucumbers | 11 | borage | 21 | chives |
| 2 | spearmint | 12 | scallions | 22 | frying peppers |
| 3 | Yellow Pear tomatoes | 13 | Chinese cabbage | 23 | cos |
| 4 | Red Plum tomatoes | 14 | dill | 24 | Oakleaf lettuce |
| 5 | bell peppers | 15 | lemon balm | 25 | Imperial lettuce |
| 6 | costmary | 16 | rocket | 26 | bibb lettuce |
| 7 | sweet cicely | 17 | escarole | 27 | white radishes |
| 8 | basil | 18 | endive | 28 | red radishes |
| 9 | tarragon | 19 | parsley | 29 | corn salad |
| 10 | upland cress | 20 | Ruby lettuce | 30 | salad burnet |

**Loose-Head Lettuce:** buy seeds, 1 packet each.

"Loose-leaf" is the name often applied to this kind of lettuce, but "loose-head" is preferable, for although the plants do not make tight balls, like iceberg, they do grow in head form.

Oakleaf, whose leaves are shaped like the leaves of oak trees, stands heat well without bolting to seed.

The red-leafed Ruby, a new variety of loose-head lettuce developed by the United States Department of Agriculture, makes a decorative note in a green salad.

**Endive:** buy seeds, 1 packet each.

The following two varieties of endive are easy to raise, and they mature toward the end of summer. Do not confuse them with French endive or Witloof chicory, which must be taken up and blanched in sand for winter use.

Green-Curled or Giant Fringed Oyster endive forms a large, dense, loose head. The leaves are finely cut, and blanch at the center. It is usually sold in the market under the name of "chicory."

Batavian endive, called escarolc in the market, is a broad-leafed endive. The large, lettuce-like leaves are slightly curled, and form round loose heads. The center leaves blanch.

**SALAD HERBS:** buy seeds, 1 packet each.

**Rocket, Roquette** (*Eruca sativa*)

An annual sweet herb of the mustard family, rocket has a strong, unique flavor. The deeply scalloped leaves grow to make a bed about 18 inches wide. Plant it early in the spring, and the leaves (the part used) come fresh all summer long, provided that the flowering stems are kept cut back. If the leaves get tough, make a second planting.

**Upland Cress** (*Barbarea præcox*)

Upland cress looks and tastes much like its cousin, water cress, but it is a bigger plant, with larger leaves. The strong peppery taste adds zest to green salads. The plants spread out to form a bed 10 or more inches in width.

This land cress is a hardy biennial and if covered with a mulch, after the ground freezes, the leaves may be used the following spring until the plant bolts, which it soon does.

**Basil** (*Ocimum Basilicum*)

This annual sweet herb belongs as much in the Garden Salad Bowl as in the Vegetable and Herb Garden. It is a must in salads which feature tomatoes, and it is equally good in green salads.

**Dill** (*Anethum graveolens*)

Dill potato salad is a change from parsley potato salad, and dill may be used to advantage in many other salads. For further notes, see **Dill** in the Vegetable and Herb Garden chapter.

**Corn Salad, Lamb's-Lettuce, Fetticus** (*Valerianella olitoria*)

Corn salad is often sold in the market under the name "field salad." The plants are small, the leaves rounded and tender and very mild in flavor. They add variety to the usual run of greens used in salads, and may also be cooked as spinach.

***Salad Burnet** (*Sanguisorba minor*)

Salad burnet is a graceful, feathery-leafed herb, with a thimble-form flower head which bears tiny rosy and white flowers about 1–2 feet above the ground. It is a perennial; the lower leaves stay green all winter under snow, but old plants tend to mat and grow poorly the second season. It is best treated as an annual, and renewed every year from seed. It is very co-operative. Once established, there is no need to buy seeds again, for salad burnet is a dependable self-sower.

Each plant requires about 1 square foot of garden space.

**Borage** (*Borago officinalis*), preferred pronunciation, first syllable to rhyme with "her."

Unless some unusual climatic condition occurs, one need buy only one packet of seeds to have a lifetime of borage. It takes a real freeze to kill the plants of this hardy annual, and in the north, borage self-sows. The seedlings appear quite early in the spring. If you must transplant them, do so while the plants are very young, for borage has a long taproot and it is difficult to transplant when old.

The young tender leaves add a cucumbery flavor to salads. When the plants reach their full height of

3 feet or better, the leaves become tough and hairy and inedible. The racemes, of small, fairy-like, rosy and pale blue star-shaped flowers, come all summer long. They look very pretty floating in a cool summer drink, and, according to folklore, bring courage to anyone who partakes of it.

Stake and tie mature plants to prevent them from sprawling on the ground.

**Parsley** (*Petroselinum hortense*)

Parsley, of course, belongs in the Garden Salad Bowl as well as in the Vegetable and Herb Garden. For further notes, see **Parsley** in Chapter 1.

**SALAD VEGETABLES:** buy seeds, 1 packet each.

**Cucumbers**

The several advantages of growing cucumbers on trellises have already been noted: they are decorative to look upon, the fruit grows perfect in form and is clean. Trellising also serves to keep the fruit from being attacked by wire worms, which sometimes happens when cucumbers lie on the ground.

They will not, however, climb of their own free will. Thc tendrils reach out eagerly in all directions, and the vines go crawling off unless they are trained to the trellises. They grow so fast that it is a good habit to visit the cucumber hills every day and tie the wayward trailers to the supports with corn string. Then the tendrils will take hold of the wood. Continue to tie until the vines have obtained their full length.

The seedsmen offer a generous variety of cucumbers from which to choose. There is the warted Burpee's Pickler, which may be used little or big; the spiny and tiny West India gherkin, good for relishes; there is the astonishing, slender China cucumber, which grows to a length of 20 inches, with a thickness of only 2 inches. There are many, more or less ordinary, plain cucumbers, with long sleek fruit.

A good sure crop for the home gardener is Burpee's Hybrid, a handsome, white-spined variety, with dark green fruit, 2½ inches in diameter and 8 inches long at maturity.

### *Scallions

Scallions are bunching onions—that is, when properly spaced, each stalk will multiply. These are small onions, popular when served raw as canapés, to dip in coarse salt. The more or less cylindrical "bulbs" are narrow and white; the tops are green. Both bottoms and tops, cut up in salads, give a mild onion flavor.

Japanese Bunching onions is a good variety. If given cover, scallions will winter over and may be harvested early, to freshen spring salads.

### Radishes

The space in the Garden Salad Bowl allows for one red and one white variety of radish. Cherry Belle is a crisp, round red radish, with white flesh. A winning point in favor of this variety is quick maturity. Given good soil, Cherry Belle will be ready to come to the table in a little better than three weeks' time after sowing.

Our choice for a white radish is Icicle. The roots

are narrow and up to 5 inches long. They are ready to eat in about a month.

Succession sowings of radishes should be made during the cool months, both spring and fall.

**Chinese or Celery Cabbage**

Chinese cabbage grows somewhat like cos lettuce, in a tall head, reaching 1½ feet in height. The leaves have a mild cabbage flavor, and are excellent either added to a green salad, shredded for coleslaw, or cooked.

Sow in the spring in climates where the summer temperature is cool. In warmer climates, do not sow until three months before the average date of the first frost. Chinese cabbage will bolt in hot weather if sown early in the spring.

Michihli is the variety usually offered by seedsmen.

**SALAD VEGETABLES:** buy plants.

**Tomatoes:** 6 plants.

In the salad garden are three Red Plum tomatoes and three Yellow Pear. For further remarks, see **Tomatoes** in the Vegetable and Herb Garden chapter.

**Peppers:** 8 plants.

Four bell peppers and four Italian frying peppers complete the vegetables in the salad garden. Both are used in green and other salads. See the Vegetable and Herb Garden chapter.

**PERENNIAL SALAD HERBS:** buy plants.

***Chives** (*Allium Schœnoprasum*): 6 clumps.

We left the chives to the last in the Vegetable and Herb Garden; we make amends by giving them first place among perennial herbs in the Garden Salad Bowl. For general information, see **Chives** in Chapter 1.

***Tarragon** (*Artemisia Dracunculus*): 6 plants.

Tarragon is as necessary in the Garden Salad Bowl as in the Vegetable and Herb Garden. See **Tarragon** in Chapter 1.

**Spearmint** (*Mentha spicata*): 4 plants.

Mint is a cool green-salad herb, also excellent in many other salads. It is a spreader and should be confined. See **Mint** in the Vegetable and Herb Garden chapter.

***Costmary, Alecost, Bible Leaf** (*Chrysanthemum Balsamita* var. *tanacetoides*)

Costmary was formerly used in making beer, which accounts for the name "alecost." A leaf of this plant was commonly used in pioneer America by church-goers, to mark the place in the Bible, hence the name "Bible leaf." Its pretty, obtuse or oblong, toothed leaves have an unusual tangy flavor. Two or three leaves give zest to a green salad.

Costmary is a rank grower. Old plants reach 5 feet

in height, but may be easily kept low by constant cutting back. It is a spreader, so confine it with a metal guard, in the manner of mint.

**Lemon Balm** (*Melissa officinalis*): 2 plants.

The leaves of lemon balm bring a cool, lemony touch to salads. See **Lemon Balm** in the Vegetable and Herb Garden chapter.

***Sweet Cicely** (*Myrrhis odorata*): 2 plants.

Young leaves of sweet cicely lend an anise flavor to salads. The crushed seeds add a similar flavor to salad dressings. The seeds, when green, are sometimes pickled.

See **Sweet Cicely,** in the Vegetable and Herb Garden chapter.

***Carpeting Thyme** (*Thymus Serpyllum*): 25 plants.

See **Carpeting Thyme** in Chapter 1.

## THE GARDEN SALAD BOWL ANNEX

We have designed this supplementary garden for the salad fancier who plans on making only the Garden Salad Bowl and who would also like to raise all the sweet herbs used in the recipes for meats, fish, vegetables, canapés, soups, and desserts in this book. These herbs are all included in the Vegetable and Herb Garden chapter, and so if you decide to make both the vegetable-herb and salad-herb gardens, the Annex will not be necessary.

In the Annex are eight choice perennial sweet herbs—namely, rosemary, origanum (sweet marjoram, if you prefer), thyme, lovage, winter savory, garden sage, pineapple sage, and hyssop;

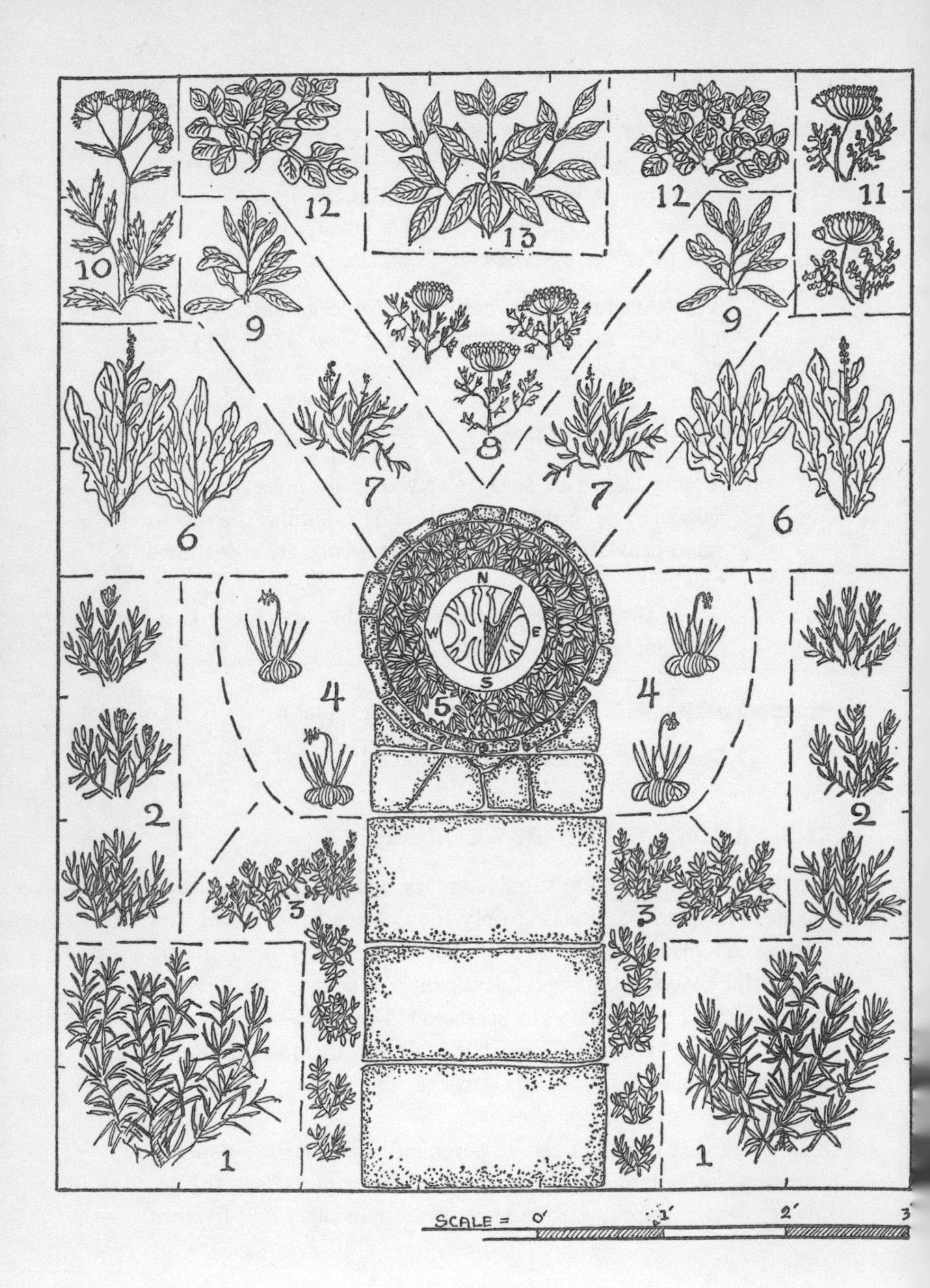

10
12
13
12
11
9
9
8
6
7
7
6
N
W
E
S
4
5
4
2
2
3
3
1
1
SCALE = 0' 1' 2' 3'

the soup herb, perennial sorrel; the biennial, chervil; the annual, coriander; and a goodly patch of those inestimably fine onions, shallots.

The alternative for the salad fancier who has no space for the Annex to the Garden Salad Bowl is to use dried herbs in recipes that call for herbs, not included in the Garden Salad Bowl, or to cut down on some of the planting in the latter garden and substitute the herbs from the Annex garden.

---

THE ANNEX TO THE GARDEN SALAD BOWL

1 Rosemary: 2 plants
2 Hyssop: 6 plants
3 Garden Thyme: 8 plants
4 Shallots: 20 bulbs
5 Carpeting Thyme: 5 plants
6 French Sorrel: 1 packet seeds
7 Winter Savory: 4 plants
8 Coriander: 1 packet seeds
9 Garden Sage: 2 plants
10 Lovage: 1 plant
11 Chervil: 1 packet seeds
12 Origanum: 2 plants
13 Pineapple Sage: 1 plant

# 3. OF GOOD GARDEN LOAM

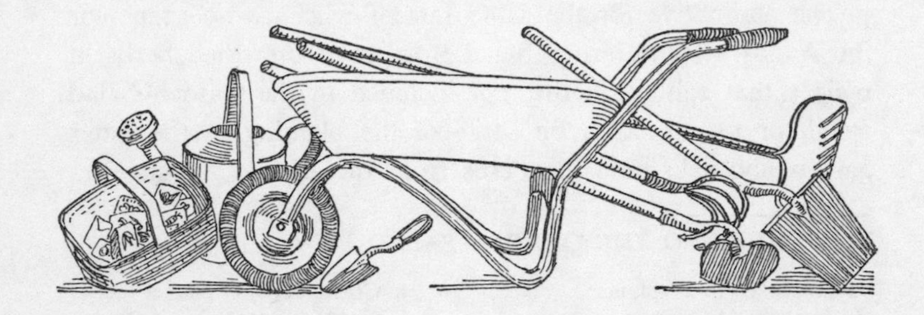

The plants are ordered; the seeds have come—they are so small, they scarcely bulge their envelopes. They belie the advance notices in the catalogues which promise miracles from the infinitesimal teaspoons of dormant life in each packet. While looking at the colored pictures in the catalogues, we had visions of bumptious squash, long, enamel-green cucumbers, busting big beets, plump, ruby-bright tomatoes, elegant, streamlined carrots. In the catalogues, the dill has burst into beautiful and correct umbelliferous blossoms; the cress and rocket have large luscious leaves which would pep up a salad, no matter how tired. Now the seeding of the summer's bounty lies within your two hands, and you wonder if you can ever make the seedsmen's promised miracles come true.

There are certain fundamental principles that help.

First comes the equipment.

## TOOLS

The editors of catalogues try to inveigle winter-weary, armchair green thumbers into ordering the latest gadgets for the garden —tools which, so they claim, will eliminate backache, abolish insects with a single "poof," and give precognition treatment to the gardener's every problem. If you have been seduced by the advertisements, you may be disappointed in our stark list, for all you actually need to prepare and maintain small gardens, such as the Vegetable and Herb Garden, the Garden Salad Bowl, and the Annex to the Salad Bowl are:

1 shovel
1 hoe
1 long-handled hand cultivator
1 trowel
1 steel rake
1 turf cutter
1 hand weeder
stakes and guideline
1 watering can and/or sprinkler
2 spray guns: one for dust, one for liquid
*and* 1 featherweight, metal wheelbarrow

A word about the wheelbarrow. The ingenuity of modern metallurgists has elevated the wheelbarrow from the heavyweight, ditchdigger class of implements, into my lady's tool shed, for even the most unathletic female can trundle the new featherweight barrow about with the greatest of ease. A standard barrow measures 25 by 31 inches. You can easily lift it completely off the ground with one hand, but in spite of its delicate feel and looks, it is rugged, it stands up under rough manhandling, and it costs under eight dollars. This barrow comes prefabricated in a number of parts, and unless you are an expert at picture puzzles, it is wise to have your hardware dealer put it together for you, particularly since he is certain to have the right wrenches required to make fast the bolts.

Of course, if you have, or can borrow, a power garden tractor, use it by all means for the initial plowing and harrowing, but such a machine is of no use thereafter in small gardens. The work may be accomplished with the hand tools listed above, without too much backache.

## THE SITE

After choosing the tools, next comes the choosing of a site for the garden. The ideal location for the Vegetable and Herb Garden, the Garden Salad Bowl, and the Annex is in full sun, but a location that receives five hours of midday sunlight may be used successfully.

If possible, locate on high rather than low ground, for good drainage is absolutely essential for growing the herbs and vegetables listed. Level land is preferable, but heavy mulching, to prevent nutrients from leaching away during rains, makes it possible to garden on even a steep slope. If you have nothing to choose from but low spots, desist and garden in pots, or fill in, build up, raise a small plot above the boggy ground, for most herbs and vegetables drown easily.

So much for sunshine and the lay of the land. Next, the quality of soil.

## DEBUNKING THE POOR-SOIL MYTH

That vegetables grow best in good garden loam has been a long-accepted truth. So do herbs.

Some writers on herbs maintain just the opposite. They say that herbs grow best in poor soil. We do not know who started this statement, but it has got into print, not once, but again and again, and it keeps going around, by word of mouth, until the poor beginner is deluded into believing that herbs really do grow best in poor soil. They don't. Like vegetables, herbs grow best in good garden loam.

This dictatorial statement stems from our own experience in trying to grow herbs in poor soil, which was all that we had in unmulched sections of our gardens, after violent hurricanes struck in our area. The torrential rain sheet eroded and gutted all the good soil away. The herbs came up, yes—little spindly things. They struggled to survive, but what there was of each of them was scarcely worth the bother to harvest.

Another illustration is seen in this quotation from a letter of a beginner who tried the poor-soil theory. She says: "I tried it in the picking garden and the plants grew about 2 inches, and then went on a strike! As it came near the time to start the chutney vinegar, which takes bushels of herbs, I became concerned."

At this point she started feeding her herb plants, and the response was "immediate and reassuring."

From another letter: "The fifty tarragon plants you sent us have burgeoned beyond our wildest dreams." This, from an herb grower who is raising tarragon in Oregon in topsoil 30 feet deep! We in the hills of New England must get along as best we can on mere inches of topsoil, and this shallow soil must be fed to get good results.

As an example of the kind of growth to be expected of herbs grown in the soil of the quality we have set as our standard, we measured the plants in a bed of rosemary, thyme, and skirrets (an old potherb) when planted in the spring; then we took height and girth at harvesttime. Thc rosemary was set out as foot-high plants grown in 5-inch pots. By the following fall, they lacked an inch of being 3 feet tall; each bush was 2 feet wide, full, handsome, lush-stemmed, sturdy, upstanding. And the aroma—*oo-la-la!* Terrific! Don't let anyone tell you that big sturdy plants have less essential oil than a spindly, stunted dwarf. Rosemary takes years to attain a good size if it is not fed.

In front of the rosemary, the row of small nursery plants

of garden thyme had, by fall, bushed out into luxuriant clumps 20 inches in diameter. Behind the rosemary, the skirrets stood up 52 inches tall, lovely bushy plants—and, of more moment to the cook, the roots (the part eaten) had grown big enough to eat. In poor soil, skirret roots look like worms. They are so tiny, it is practically impossible to cut out the woody core, which must be removed before serving.

In a nearby bed, under the same treatment, the stems of the tarragon were ½ inch in diameter at ground level; each plant covered a good square foot in area. The stems were well leafed out, and very aromatic.

To produce these satisfying results, we dug into the ground a generous amount of well-rotted stable manure and fed the plants once a week with homemade liquid manure.

## LIQUID MANURE

This wrinkle of feeding plants must be as old as gardening itself. At least every Old World gardener we have met swears by it. To make liquid manure, take a discarded laundry tub or a similar container, partly fill it with water; fill a burlap sack with fresh cow manure and let it soak in the tub for a day, now and then stirring the water by swishing the bag around in the tub. Water the plants with this solution once a week.

It is advisable to use up all the liquid each time and dump the solid matter out of the bag onto the compost pile. If the manure is left wet in the tub for long, maggots hatch.

Now we have, we hope, sufficiently proved that herbs grow best in fertile soil. We return to specific data for preparing soil for the three gardens of this book.

## PREPARATION OF THE GARDENS

If gardeners could be choosers, they would ask for a good sandy loam in which to plant the Vegetable and Herb Garden, the Garden Salad Bowl and Annex. For this is the kind of soil that suits both the herbs and vegetables listed. If your soil is heavy and clayey, lighten it by digging in organic matter and coarse sand.

Next, choose the fertilizer you will use. We recommend above all others well-rotted stable manure, or chicken manure. Use much less of the latter, because chicken manure is generally much higher in certain nutrients. Stake out the outline of the garden—in the fall, if possible—and spread on the manure.

It is of course impossible to tabulate exact amounts of fertilizer for Everyman's garden. Soils differ greatly from region to region. The following table assumes that your garden is in fertile condition and of good tilth. The amounts suggested are the breakfast, luncheon, and dinner the crops will need for the current year. If your soil is poor, you will have to add more organic fertilizer. In the following table the superphosphate supplements the phosphate in the stable manure, and the 5-10-10 adds some potash, a nutrient in which poultry manure is low.

**The Vegetable and Herb Garden:** 25 by 25 feet

⅓ ton well-rotted stable manure
15 pounds superphosphate
OR
5 bushels poultry manure
4½ pounds 5-10-10 commercial fertilizer

**The Bed of Peas and Squash:** 5 by 25 feet

125 pounds stable manure
3 pounds superphosphate
OR
1 bushel poultry manure
1 pound 5-10-10 commercial fertilizer

**The Garden Salad Bowl:** 18 by 13 feet

about 250 pounds well-rotted stable manure
5 pounds superphosphate
OR
2 bushels poultry manure
1½ pounds 5-10-10 commercial fertilizer

**The Annex to the Garden Salad Bowl:** 9 by 7 feet

63 pounds well-rotted stable manure
1¾ pounds superphosphate
OR
½ bushel poultry manure
½ pound 5-10-10 commercial fertilizer

Good rich compost has about the same fertilizer value as, and may be substituted for, or used in conjunction with, stable manure. Dried cow or sheep manure is also good. Wood ashes from soft woods add 2 per cent, and from hard woods, 8 per cent of potash, and some lime.

It seems hardly necessary to warn anyone about using too much manure in this age of modern farming when every bit of cow manure goes, not into a pit, but fresh from the barn cleaner, via the manure spreader, out onto the cow pasture or the cornfield. The thought that one might have too much is merely a dream. The wish is only to get your shovel into some. But, even of good things, there can be too much. All the leafy vegetables and herbs need plenty of nitrogen, a nutrient found in stable and chicken manure. Nitrogen is especially rich in the latter. Too much nitrogen could bring about too leafy a growth in tomatoes and lessen fruiting. Therefore, every three years have your soil tested to be sure that it is in balance and not overloaded with any one element.

A soil test is especially necessary to determine whether or not you need lime. Your state experiment station or agricultural college may supply you with containers in which to collect the soil, and with instructions on how to take soil samples.

In the place where you are asked to list the crops to be raised, just say that you want your pH* to be 6.5. The pH recommended for soils in a vegetable garden is 6–6.5, and herbs grow well in a soil with a pH 6.5–pH 7.2. So 6.5 is the pH best for the combination Vegetable and Herb Garden or the Garden Salad Bowl. In the Annex, a garden of herbs only, jack up the pH to 7.0 or 7.2.

If your soil tests at less than 6.5, spread on quick-acting, hydrated lime, in the amount recommended by the soil test.

## CAUTION—GO SLOW

An advantage of using organic fertilizer such as stable manure or compost is that, along with the nutrients so necessary to plant growth, they add humus to the soil and improve its tilth.

The numbered fertilizers, such as 5-10-5 and 5-10-10, contain the three principal elements necessary for plant growth: nitrogen, phosphorus, and potash, in that order. These chemical fertilizers should be thought of as vitamin pills, or a shot in the arm. They give the plants a boost. The nitrogen is used up in the course of a year's growth. Phosphorus and potash may not necessarily be used up in a year.

A vital point to remember is that these fertilizers are strong. Use too much, or apply them too close to the plants, and fertilizer burn will result. You may even kill the crop.

The best way to apply a chemical fertilizer in the home garden during the growing season is to "line it out"—that is, sprinkle it along each row, 2–3 inches from the plants, at the rate of about 1 pound to a 50-foot row, and work it carefully into the soil.

Nitrogen, phosphorus, and potash are not, of course, the only elements essential to good plant growth. The trace elements—

* pH is a symbol used to denote the degree of acidity or alkalinity of soils. 7 is neutral. More than 7 is alkaline, or "sweet"; less than 7 is acid, or "sour."

boron, to mention one—are also necessary, but in *extremely* small quantities. Most commercial fertilizers do not contain trace elements in the analysis, but you may buy those that do. However, soils in many regions have sufficient amounts of these trace elements to make it unnecessary to apply these in addition to organic manure or to a commercial fertilizer such as 5-10-5. So unless you live in a locality where the soil is known to be deficient in one of the minor elements, forget the matter. Chances are that your plants, when fed as suggested, will prosper. If they do not, then have a soil test made to determine what the deficiency is.

Once again the warning: the numbered fertilizers should not be applied willy-nilly. So garden it safe; keep on the organic side as far as possible.

## PLOWING

The best time for plowing, which for those without a power garden tractor means turning over the soil with a spade, is in the fall. This should be done after the manure has been spread. Dig it all in, leaving the earth rough. Do not harrow—rake, to you—until spring, but allow the soil to lie fallow. This gives the rains and snow a chance to leach the nutrients into the soil. If your garden is on a slope, throw on a heavy mulch before winter comes, or most of the good plant food will wash away down yonder, where it won't do you any good.

Come spring, remove the mulch (if any), rake the beds out sleek and smooth, then set out stakes and the guideline.

## WHEN TO PLANT

This is a tricky question to answer. There are so many elements involved, and dominating them all is that great, omnipotent dictator, the weather.

No one would deny that peas should go in as early as the ground can be worked, but to give a date, at least in our temperamental New England climate, would be foolhardy.

Jottings from our country journal—Sunday, April 3, 1955: "It began to snow. By Monday morning, storm over, 22 inches had fallen, nearly 2 feet of heavy wet mush; it weighted down the garage roof so that the door lock jammed.

"Shoveled snow off roof, for fear it might collapse. Telephone and power out.

"In midafternoon a huge bank of snow came crawling down the road. Behind it was Barry on his bulldozer. He had tried to plow us out with his big farm tractor—got stuck. He pushed our car up the hill with the blade of the bulldozer so that we could get back to New York."

That year we could not plow our main garden until May 15. But we planted peas on April 23 in a sunny spot, southern exposure, where the snow had melted and the ground had dried out sufficiently to be worked.

The rule, then, for planting peas is simple: Get them in just as soon as you can. They are a cool-weather crop.

One year we tried planting them in the fall—a perfectly satisfactory date, save for one drawback. The field mice somehow discovered the row, and by spring they had eaten at least half of the peas sown.

So we have given up fall planting of peas, and plant them, along with other cool-weather crops, as early as the ground can be worked. Don't make the mistake of planting in wet soil. The ground must dry out until the soil is friable. Then plant peas, lettuce, endive, red cabbage, kohlrabi, carrots, beets, Swiss chard, shallots, scallions, and, in areas where the summers are cool, Chinese cabbage. Parsley, chervil, and dill may also be planted early. A dependable rule is to plant the other seeds listed for the Vegetable and Herb Garden and the Garden Salad Bowl and Annex just after the final date for a killing frost is expected in your locality.

In our locality, it is traditional to plant vegetable and herb seeds, except for the cool-weather crops, and to set out the nursery plants on Memorial Day. Actually we rarely get a killing frost after May 15, and some years when the month of April smiles upon us, we get adventurous, take a sporting chance, and set out even the tomato plants two weeks before May 30. With luck, we have a flying head start, but often, even if the days and nights are frost free, the vegetable seeds rot and the plants stand still, or recede; for the ground is still cold and wet, and lacks the hospitable warmth most seeds and plants need in the spring to start them thriftily on their way.

## HOW DEEP TO PLANT; HOW THICK TO SOW

Cover tiny seeds, such as sweet marjoram, with a mere sprinkle of soil; then pat them down. Plant carrots at a depth of ½ inch in sandy loam, ¼ inch in heavy soil. Make a little trench about 1 inch deep for beets.

We prefer to plant seeds thick enough to sustain some loss to cutworms, rather than use cutworm bait.

Broadcast peas generously along a trench about 1½ inches deep in sandy loam, a little shallower in heavy soil, and do not thin.

Place the snap beans 2 inches apart in a trench similar to the one for peas; poke eight to ten squash and cucumber seeds into each squash and cucumber hill, spacing the seeds about 2 inches apart. Cover them with about ¾ inch of soil. Thin the snap beans to 4 inches apart in the row, and the squash and cucumbers to the best four plants in each hill, after the danger of cutworms is past.

Thinning of other seeded vegetables and herbs must not be postponed too long, or damage may result to both root and leaf crops. A few, such as corn salad and chervil, do not mat, and need not be thinned. Dill is also best grown thick. The tall stems support each other. But if leaves of plants such as lettuce and sorrel overlap, and there is a rainy spell, the leaves rot; and crowded roots of plants such as turnips and carrots invite invasion of wire worms, and the roots grow in distorted shapes. So make the first thinning of root vegetables, lettuce, and most sweet herbs early. From the second thinning you will get some choice young baby carrots and beets, the first salad greens, and a teaspoon or so of first pickings of parsley, basil, and other aromatic herbs.

Following are a few specific examples of spacing between plants in rows, in the final thinning in the Vegetable and Herb Garden.

fennel: 6 inches
chard: 6 inches
okra: 18 inches
carrots: 1 inch
beets: 2–3 inches
sorrel: 8 inches
parsley: 4–6 inches

IN THE GARDEN SALAD BOWL

head lettuce: 1 foot
loose-head lettuce: 6 inches–1 foot
Chinese cabbage: 6 inches
scallions: 1 inch

A note on parsley and chervil. The seeds of these two sweet herbs are slow to germinate. To hasten germination, soak them overnight in water before planting.

Space the nursery-started plants, the tomatoes, the peppers, the tarragon, the rosemary, and the others equidistant from one another in the space allotted in the garden designs, which are marked off to scale. For example: the Vegetable and Herb Garden calls for twelve tomato plants; the space for tomatoes is 18 feet; so space each plant 1½ feet from its neighbor.

## THE VIRTUES OF MULCHING

Notes from our country journal—Thursday, August 18, 1957: "Rain began today with a backlash from Hurricane Diane, which the weather bureau had pronounced dead, at sea.

"A hose was still siphoning off the foot of water which Hurricane Connie had left in our cellar the week before. The ground was waterlogged; it had absorbed all it could hold. If any more rain fell, where could it go?"

We soon found out.

Friday, August 19: "Rain heavy; continues all night."

Next morning we heard something bump in our cellar. Investigating, we found jars of honey and mustard and crocks of vinegar floating around and around in rising waters.

The upper rows of perennial herbs in the main garden, which is on a steep slope, came through the two hurricanes in good shape; the topsoil was held snug and safe throughout the violent runoff by a deep mulch. The condition of the lower half of the garden, which was planted on the contour but not mulched, was shocking to see. The storms had been so fierce, the rain so heavy and constant, that contour planting alone had not prevented erosion. The lower parts of the field had suffered both sheet and gully erosion; there were little stony channels. This unmulched area looked more like a gravel pit than a garden. The roots of many of the perennial plants were exposed.

It took several years to replace what hurricanes Connie and Diane stole from us. Thus we learned the hard way never to leave a smidgen of sloping ground without proper cover.

A mulch is valuable for several reasons, even in gardens

planted on level ground. It keeps down weeds, conserves moisture, and eventually rots into organic matter that adds humus and nutrients to the soil.

Apply a mulch to the plants set in the Vegetable and Herb Garden, the Garden Salad Bowl and Annex as soon as they are planted. Make sure the soil is wet before the application. If there has been no rain recently, soak the soil with a hose. Mulch the seeded rows as soon as the seedlings are up about 3 inches. Meanwhile keep down the weeds with hand tools.

And put the mulch on thick, so that it will be about 3–4 inches deep when it settles; otherwise the pesky weeds will stick their heads up through the straw, or whatever you use. It is very discouraging to go to the trouble and expense of mulching and still have weeds.

The variety of mulches to choose from is legion. We mention first, our favorites, peat, and salt-marsh hay. They bring in no noxious weed seeds which might sprout, and they—particularly the peat—are very neat-looking. We prefer the Michigan type of peat to the imported. The dark, American peat is in a more advanced stage of decomposition than the imported kinds we have seen, and absorbs rain water better.

You do not have to afford these rather expensive materials. We also use any old kind of hay, or organic mulch that we can dicker for.

One year we made a deal with a lawn maintenance man who had been carting all the leaves he raked to the town dump. We arranged for him to deliver the leaves at the herb farm instead, for two dollars the small dump truckload.

We spread the leaves in the fall between three 150-foot rows of tarragon. We are of two minds about the results. Quite a few blew away before a rain wetted them down. Then the blowing stopped, but the leaves started drifting down onto the crowns of the plants. This was all right as long as the ground remained frozen, but once the tarragon began to sprout in the spring, it took careful handwork to remove the leaves without damaging the tender young tarragon sprouts. Now we dump all the leaves we get onto the compost pile.

Another time we bought a whole field of spoiled hay, if not for a song, at least for a small sum. It came about this way. In the middle of winter we passed by a neighboring farm, and there in a field was the baled hay, still lying on the ground. Upon inquiry, we found that this hay, spoiled during a prolonged summer rainy spell, had been sold to a ski-jump operator, to act as a bumper to check the skiers at the end of the runoff. The ski-jump operator had failed to take up his option, and in the spring the farmer said to us, "Take it away." We let no grass grow under our feet and we got the whole eighty-two bales for the cost of sending a trucker after them.

This was an excellent buy. The hay, already half rotted, looked like manure, and the weeds which could have been in it apparently had also rotted.

If you use wood chips, feed the plants with nitrate of soda or some other form of nitrogen; for while the little beneficial soil microbes are busy reducing the chips to compost, they rob the soil of nitrogen, which must be replaced, or the plants will be nitrogen hungry.

## STAKING

The support for the peas—brush or a chicken-wire fence—should of course be put up soon after the peas break ground. Stake the tomatoes and the pole Limas, and set the trellises for the cucumbers, right after the mulch is spread. Don't wait until the plants are ready to climb, for by then they will have a big root growth, and digging around them will damage the roots.

Tie the vines of tomatoes, pole Limas, and cucumbers to train them to climb. We prune staked tomatoes to one stem and pinch off suckers, to produce bigger fruit.

## THE ENEMY

Some people tell you that the essential oils in herbs ward off all pests and diseases. They say that if you plant pennyroyal, you won't have mosquitoes. This does not work, nor are herbs immune to common garden pests, which the vegetable grower must battle. Perhaps credulity about the immunity theory developed during the decline of herb growing in America, when herb gardens were so few and far apart that pests did not find them. In any case, part of your summer work will be to protect both the herbs and the vegetables in your combination gardens from invasions of microbes, assorted chewing and sucking insects, and monstrous rodents.

Whenever we see even one small woodchuck, we react the way a fireman does to a four-alarm fire: the cry goes out, "Find the hole!"—for there are only two things to do about a woodchuck. One is to shoot it and the other is to find its hole, drop in a can of Cyanogas, and cover the entrance with dirt at once. We have got positively stony-hearted on the subject of woodchucks. One simply cannot have a garden of vegetables, lettuce, and herbs and be kind to woodchucks.

One modest-sized woodchuck will mow down a whole row of lettuce as neatly as a power mower; it will do the same to a row of origanum. A woodchuck's appetite is catholic. They eat practically everything that grows in an herb or vegetable garden. One once ate two thirds of a large Hubbard squash at one sitting. The only things that they have not touched in our garden are tarragon, tomatoes, and sage.

There is, however, a way that you can live and let live with the other rodent-like pest, rabbits.

## DRIED BLOOD

Rabbits are dainty feeders. They do not, like woodchucks, mow; they merely nibble. And if rabbits were as few in numbers as woodchucks, one could afford to be generous. But where there is one rabbit, you may be sure that there are, or soon will be, more. A half dozen nibblers working together on a bed of salad burnet—one of their favorite dishes—will ruin the burnet for the season. What to do? Go to your garden-supply shop and buy dried blood.

Sprinkle a thin line of dried blood around all the favorite rabbit food in the Vegetable and Herb Garden, and the Garden Salad Bowl—the burnet, lettuce, any of the cabbage family, and carrots, of course. The rabbits will stay meekly on the lawn and eat clover.

The only hitch about this is that rain washes away the smell and you have to put more dried blood out after every good shower, which in a way is a dual blessing, for dried blood is good organic fertilizer.

Whether dried blood works to stop woodchucks, we cannot say. A woodchuck is such a glutton, one experiment could be fatal to a whole row of beans.

## OF BUGS AND SUCH

We have noticed in our experience that diseases and insects attack weak plants in preference to strong, healthy specimens. The Department of Agriculture has recently been experimenting to find out why, but whatever the reason, it is true.

Even healthy plants, however, are subject to attack by insects and may be infected by fungi and other diseases.

Notes from the country journal—July 7, 1957: "Hot, dry again; picked first 2 Jap. beetles."

July 18: "Picked 18 Jap. beetles. Caught 3 katydids on the roses, chewing buds."

In the small combination gardens featured in this book, several big insects, such as those mentioned above, can be kept well under control by hand picking into a small can partly filled with kerosene.

Most of the other insects which in our experience have attacked both herbs and vegetables, can be controlled by regular spraying with rotenone or pyrethrum, dust or spray. These are non-toxic insecticides. For mildew, use sulfur, which is also non-poisonous to humans, but keep it out of the eyes.

## SUMMER ADVANCES

The peas are gone. The lush summer harvest comes. Squash and cucumbers are ripening on the vines. Tomatoes turn red, the salad is heading, and the time comes to make succession plantings, to fill in the gaps.

In the Vegetable and Herb Garden, make second plantings of beets and carrots, to assure a fall crop.

In the Garden Salad Bowl, make a second planting of Green Curled endive and escarole (Broad-Leaf Batavian endive), radishes and corn salad. Replace the early bibb lettuce and the Ruby with Slobolt, a heat-resistant variety of lettuce. The outer leaves of Slobolt may be picked and the plants will grow new leaves for the rest of the season.

A note on fennel. To blanch, bank up the bulblike leaf stems with earth.

Now, if the gardener has prepared the soil well, if the mulch lies good and deep, he should more or less rest on his shovel. There is little to do for the rest of the season. Water during droughts and spray when necessary. For the remainder of the summer, enjoy the bounty of vegetables, lettuce, and herbs grown in good garden loam.

And on a leisurely summer's afternoon invite your fellow gardeners to come and see the results of your labors. For refreshment serve them the old British favorite, Pimm's Cup, with herbs.

Not too much is known about the Mr. Pimm, for whom this venerable drink was named, but it is certain that, years ago, he owned a restaurant in Cheapside, London. It was then the custom for a restaurateur to name a famous drink of the house after his restaurant. The earliest known record of Pimm's Cup dates from the year 1859 and the name first appears in a newspaper article in a report on a shipment of the beverage to the troops in Egypt, during the Egyptian campaign, in the year 1898.

There are now on the market five different Pimm's Cups, each with a different base, and each served with a variety of garnishes, from cucumber strips to maraschino cherries. In England the cucumber-flavored borage is a favorite herbal garnish.

### PIMM'S CUP A LA HEMLOCK HILL

spearmint sprigs
lemon-balm sprigs
Pimm's Cup No. 1 (gin base)
ice cubes
club soda
borage flowers
salad-burnet sprigs

Serve in old-fashioned or highball glasses.

Rub the inside of each glass thoroughly with a sprig of mint, then with a sprig of lemon balm, and discard. Measure 1 jigger Pimm's into each glass, add ice cubes, and fill glass with club soda. Float two or three borage flowers in each drink, and stir. Garnish each glass with a sprig of salad burnet. The aroma as well as the taste is very cool and stimulating.

# 4. ON THE TERRACE AND THE WINDOW SHELF

## A RING-POT HERB GARDEN

For gardeners with limited or no garden space, containers offer a charming setting in which to grow herbs. A delightful way to raise herbs in summer, on a terrace or a porch, is in imported terra rosa ring pots.

Potters in Italian hill towns, spurning machine methods, hand mold the native reddish clay; skillfully they turn the classic ring-pot form, in sizes ranging from 8 inches in diameter, 7 inches deep, to big estate jardinieres, so big (40 inches in diameter, 3 feet deep) that it would seem that a derrick be required to hoist them about.

The unglazed, soft-textured, rosy-tinged pots are decorative even when empty. They are much more so when planted with aromatic herbs, thus ready at hand for the cook to snip and to use as needed for flavoring goodies from canapés to angel frappé. And as one watches the herbs grow in these pots, one easily imagines that they feel at home and derive comfort, if not actual nourishment, from this suitable environment. Most culinary herbs are themselves native to the terra rosa soil of the Mediterranean region. In any case, herbs flourish in these pots—even temperamental tarragon, *if* you set it in a pot of the proper size.

Anyone who has tried to coax tarragon to grow in the small pot in which it is commonly offered at a nursery knows how hopeless the effort is. Tarragon exists, yes, but instead of growing, the stems contrarily shrink, in spite of all administrations, if the plant is long contained in a 5-inch pot. Just transplant it to a terra rosa pot, 12 inches in diameter, and you will be amazed at the results.

The reason, of course, is fundamentally the matter of pot size, for tarragon roots grow shallow. They reach out on all sides near the surface of the soil, and they must have room to stretch their toes. Native clay sentiment aside, tarragon will also do well in a container of similar size to the ring pot suggested, even if it is made of common clay, or other suitable plant container material. (See Of Tubs.)

So if you would grow tarragon beyond the garden proper, the first consideration is: Make the container big enough. The same is true, to a lesser degree, of the mints, which do make satisfactory growth for a short period of time in small pots, but will grow luxuriantly all summer long in 12-by-10-inch ring pots.

With the multitude of herbs in our open garden at Hemlock Hill, it might seem redundant for us to have herbs on a terrace.

Still, we like to grow a selection, for the decorative value and for handiness: at least one ring pot of tarragon, one of spearmint, one with a big handsome rosemary plant, and one with a plant of true myrtle.

True myrtle (*Myrtus communis*)—not to be confused with the "cemetery myrtle" or periwinkle (*Vinca*)—is a beautiful house plant with small, vital-looking, shiny leaves and delicate frothy white flowers. It cannot stand cold weather and so must be brought indoors at the first hint of frost. Its seeds are used to a limited extent for their flavor, but the plant is best known, and most often grown, as a "folklore" herb. A bouquet of true myrtle is customarily carried for good luck by brides of Eastern Europe. The bride takes a cutting from the bouquet, and if the cutting roots successfully, then, the saying goes, the marriage is certain to be a happy one.

## A BAKER'S DOZEN RING POTS

With ample space on the terrace or porch a complete basic perennial herb garden may be grown in ring pots. Start with plants (not seeds), and plant one plant to a 12-inch pot:

tarragon
lemon balm
spearmint
origanum
pineapple sage

These herbs spread rapidly and will soon fill their pots.

A single good-sized plant (at least a foot tall), also to a single 12-by-10-inch ring pot:

garden sage
sweet cicely
lovage
rosemary

If you are an impatient gardener—and we are—it is advisable to start with three plants (nursery size) to each 12-inch ring pot for the following:

garden thyme
chives
hyssop
winter savory

Single nursery-sized plants of these herbs look lonesome in big ring pots. As the garden thyme and chives spread, however (which they will), and as the hyssop branches out, it will perhaps become necessary to reduce the number of plants in each 12-inch ring pot to one.

The obvious alternative is to plant the four last-named plants—garden thyme, chives, hyssop, and winter savory—one each in smaller, 8-inch ring pots.

All the herbs mentioned in the baker's-dozen ring-pot garden, with the exception of chives, the sages, and sweet cicely, have inconspicuous flowers. Sweet cicely has decorative white umbels of flowers, succeeded by decorative dark seeds. Chives bear pretty light purple blossoms, but it is unlikely that those in your garden of pots will bloom, for you will be cutting the plants back continuously for use in the kitchen. Common sage also has pretty purple flowers. One variety has decorative white blossoms. The blossoms of pineapple sage are crimson. But the sages bloom for only a short time, and therefore, if you would lend a dash of brightness to your otherwise gray-green color scheme, add two 12-inch ring pots of annuals. Fill one with nasturtiums, and the second with calendulas, known to herb growers as pot marigolds. Both of these blossom all summer long. Use the peppery leaves of the nasturtiums as a substitute for upland cress, and the flowers of calendulas to give a yellow color and a slight flavor to stews and ragouts. Buy the old-fashioned, single-flowered nasturtiums, if possible, for they are the ones traditionally raised in herb gardens.

Nasturtiums and calendulas must of course be started from seeds, and if you want to get the pots going early on the terrace, they should be started indoors. Growing seedlings in the average overheated house is a tricky business. Seedlings need a moist, temperature-controlled, greenhouse environment. Odds are that seedlings raised at home will lack vigor. So unless you yourself have a greenhouse, a conservatory, or at least a cold frame, or unless you are that rare indoor green-thumb gardener, and can coax plants to grow anywhere (in which case you will overcome the odds against you), you had better buy the seeds and ask your local greenhouse man to start the nasturtiums and pot marigolds for you in flats. He understands the timing and will have the seedlings of the right size for transplanting when frost-free days permit you to set them in the pots out-of-doors.

## FOR THE NARROW LEDGE

Although most herbs are happier in big containers, gardeners with a space problem can grow a selected number in pots 5 inches in diameter. Among those which will do well in smaller containers are chives, small plants of rosemary (about 6–7 inches tall), small plants of garden sage—but not pineapple sage, which gets big too fast. Small lemon balm, winter savory, hyssop, and mint will likewise do well. Try also a pot of garden thyme, sweet marjoram or origanum, and basil. Basil, an annual, must of course be started from seeds.

Dill grows too tall, summer savory too spindly, for small containers; and tarragon, remember, never, *never,* in a space that cramps the roots.

## NOW, TO POT

If you use clay pots, heed the old gardener's rule. If they are new, set them to soak for a quarter of an hour in water, to saturate the clay. Scrub old pots with a stiff brush and water (no soap), to remove dirt and moss.

A cardinal point to remember in potting herbs is that these plants must have good drainage in order to grow well in a natural setting, and in the unnatural environment of a container, good drainage is even more important. Herbs potted with inadequate drainage promptly drown.

To avoid waterlogging, follow the traditional method. Break up an old clay pot and arrange pieces of the broken pot over the holes in the pot to be planted. Then, in a 5-inch pot, spread a handful of coarse gravel around and over the shards. Add a good inch of gravel over the shards in a 12-by-10-inch pot.

If the location where you set the pots is absolutely flat, it will be necessary to elevate them with a splinter or two of wood, so that excess water can get out of the drainage hole and from under the bottom of the pot.

Next, the soil. There are probably as many different formulas for potting soil as there are gardeners. A potting mixture we find good for herbs:

3 parts good garden loam
2 parts compost, or good leaf mold, or American granulated peat moss
1 part sharp sand

To a bushel of this mixture add a pint of well-rotted stable manure or a half pint dried sheep manure. Work it all together well.

To plant, arrange drainage material and partially fill pot with potting soil. Set the plant in the container and gently firm more soil around the roots, making certain not to cramp them, or to cover the crown. The soil should come within about a half inch of the top of a 5-inch container, and to within about an inch of the top of a 12-by-10-inch pot. Sprinkle well with water and keep in the shade until the plant takes hold.

Special care should be taken in planting tarragon, for the roots break easily.

## OF TUBS

The herbs listed for a garden of ring pots can as well be raised in decorative wooden tubs, preferably made of wood that naturally resists wet-soil rot. Heart redwood is toxic to the fungi which rots wood in contact with wet soil. Cypress is another wet-soil-rot-resistant wood. Garden-supply shops stock several sizes of the rosy-hued heart redwood and natural-colored blond cypress tubs, in handsome octagonal design bound with metal bands. The 12-inch (diameter)-by-11-inch (depth) tub is ample for growing the herbs suggested for the 12-inch ring pots, and makes a particularly good container for raising tarragon and mint. These tubs cost less than the ring pots.

An attractive, though expensive, variation on the redwood-cypress-and-terra-rosa color scheme is a tub of nut-brown Java teak, another wood toxic to the fungi which causes most woods to rot when in contact with wet soil. The teak tubs we speak of are handmade and imported from Holland by White Flower Farm, Litchfield, Connecticut. They come in an indoor and outdoor style. They are, like the redwood and cypress tubs, joined by metal bands, and they range in size from 8–14 inches in diameter.

Still another octagonal tub, an indoor-outdoor bucket, is made of pine, finished in maple, walnut, white or black, and waxed and waterproofed.

## PLANTER BOXES

A window box, now generally referred to as a planter box, has the advantage of being able to hold more than one species of herbs in the single container. Planter boxes are still most commonly made in the oblong, window-box design. Imaginative dealers also stock assorted shapes—square, round, hexagonal, and triangular—for planter boxes are suitable for use not only on window sills but also on stone walls, on steps, along the edges of flagstone paths, and in similar locations. A gardener may choose to arrange several shapes, to make his own group planter-box design. The material? Not metal, unless you plan to use another container inside, leaving an air space between.

One is not surprised to find that beginners are misled into thinking that metal is a good material for a plant container, for stacks of metal window boxes are carried by many garden-supply shops and, from time to time, appear among the baked goods and other victuals in supermarkets, and amid the plethora of non-drug articles stocked by modern "drug" stores. But metal is a poor material for a plant container, because it heats up too much in the sun.

A superior material for window or other planter boxes is the same as that used for some of the best plant tubs—namely, wood. A commercial planter box in window-box design suitable for growing a small assortment of herb plants is a redwood box, measuring 32 inches long, 7 inches deep, and 8¾ inches wide.

A box of this size will nourish a miniature herb garden as follows: one 12-inch rosemary plant; one small (6-inch plant) garden sage; one nursery-size origanum; one garden thyme, and two parsley plants.

To plant a window box, use same drainage material and potting mixture as for potted herbs.

## IF YOU LIKE TO DO IT YOURSELF

The California Redwood Association, 576 Sacramento Street, San Francisco, California, issues a free folder with designs for and information on how to put together planter boxes of redwood. It is not necessary to finish redwood to preserve it. As has been said, the heart redwood (but *not* the sapwood) resists wet-soil rot, and when left to weather, slowly darkens, then turns to a pleasing driftwood-gray. For those who wish to hurry nature's weathering, bleaches are advised. Instructions are included in the redwood folder on how to finish this wood in the rosy hue in which many commercial redwood tubs and planter boxes are finished.

Cypress and cedar are also good, naturally durable woods to use for home-planter-box ventures, but the less expensive, though less soil-rot-resistant, common pine boards may be used.

Whatever the wood, select stout boards, at least ¾ inch thick. Thin boards are liable to crack and warp. To prevent rusting, use brass screws for fastening.

Good minimum dimensions for the homemade window box are the 32-inch-long commercial redwood planter box mentioned above. We have tried smaller boxes for herbs—in fact we put one on the market, but it proved satisfactory only for the littlest herbs such as sweet marjoram and thyme, and even these do better in the bigger box.

After you have fastened your homemade box together, drill two rows of drainage holes, each ½ inch in diameter, and spaced ½ foot from its neighbor, one row down each side of the bottom of the box.

Note that a professionally designed planter box or tub is elevated, so that the bottom does not rest flat upon the floor. Copy this in your homemade box by fastening two small cleats on the bottom. This serves a dual purpose. It combats heat by permitting air to circulate underneath the box and helps prevent clogging of the drainage holes.

Tubs and planter boxes made of pine will last longer if painted. To prevent harm to the plants, do not set them in the box until the paint is thoroughly dry. If you prefer to finish with a wood preservative, make certain that the preservative you use is not toxic to plants. Cuprinol will not harm plants, if the treated container is allowed to dry well, out-of-doors, before planting. Caution should be observed when applying this preservative. The horticulturist at the Brooklyn Botanical Garden advises, "Be sure to wear gloves and long sleeves, and try not to get your face splashed. . . . It burns but doesn't show up until the next day."

## FOR FREE

Are you shopping around for a ready-made, no-cost-to-you container in which to grow a miniature herb garden? See the dairy clerk at your supermarket and ask him to save you a wooden cheese box. We refer to the round boxes in which wheels of Cheddar and similar cheeses are packed for shipment from the cheese processor. They come in many different sizes, from those not so big as an alarm clock to tall, barrel-sized drums. A cheese box 16 inches in diameter and 6½ inches deep is a good size to use for an herb plant box.

To transform the cheese container into one for plants, drill a circle of seven holes, each ½ inch in diameter and about 2 inches from the outer edge of the bottom of the box, for drainage.

The wood of cheese boxes is thin and splintery, and it is therefore more practical to elevate the cheese box, simply by setting two small loose cleats under the box, rather than trying to nail cleats to the bottom.

You may leave your converted cheese box the natural wood

color, but it will last longer if you paint or "Cuprinol" it. Make sure, of course, that the paint or preservative is thoroughly dry before using the box for plants.

In this "convertible," plant a clump of sweet marjoram, one of chives, one plant of winter savory, one of garden thyme, with a small rosemary for center accent.

Prepare drainage and potting soil as for regular planter boxes.

## PERMANENT TERRACE BOXES

Permanent terrace boxes may be made of expensive materials—marble or polished granite—in which case, of course, a professional stonemason's services will be required. Or they may be homemade, of inexpensive and easy-to-handle brick and cinder or cement blocks. These large, roomy permanent boxes simulate the effect of a small garden, and herbs grow well in them. They also offer, even to country people with ample garden space, an attractive way to raise culinary herbs close by the kitchen or the dining-room door, where they may be snipped and used conveniently.

If the bricks and blocks are cemented together, they should have a good foundation, to prevent heaving during freezing weather in winter. One can, however, lay up a dry wall of common gray cinder blocks and paint them with Bondex, a waterproof cement paint, which comes in white, green, and other colors, and the effect is pleasing.

The terrace box at our own kitchen door measures 64 inches long by 24 inches wide (outside measurement). It is made on a dry-laid (no cement) fieldstone terrace, and one side of the box is formed by the kitchen wall.

Materials required:

6 cinder or cement blocks (8 by 8 by 16 inches)
25 common red bricks
2 10-quart pails rubble
1 quart dry sheep manure
3 pails sharp sand
good garden loam
Bondex

Set the cement or cinder blocks as per diagram. Paint them on the outside only with Bondex, as per directions on the package, and top the blocks with the bricks. Scatter the rubble over the bottom of the box, spread sand on the rubble, then fill the box to within an inch of the top of the bricks with garden loam, and mix in the sheep manure. Plant the following plants:

2 tarragon
2 garden thyme
2 parsley
1 spearmint
1 winter savory
1 garden sage
1 origanum
1 large clump chives
1 rosemary

If you set a permanent box direclty on the ground, and not on stonework, then you may substitute a lovage plant for a tarragon plant, if you wish. Lovage has such a long taproot, it will not usually grow well unless it can grow deep into the earth.

Our second cinder-block-and-red-brick terrace box is designed to grow potted herbs on an open terrace, under a roofed porch, where the box gets sun at least half the day. Outside measurement—length, 8 feet; width, 32 inches; height, 26 inches.

The materials:

42 cinder blocks (8 by 8 by 16 inches)
60 bricks
sand
Bondex
18 herb plants in 6-inch pots
2 herb plants in 10-inch pots

Lay the cinder blocks as per diagram, paint with Bondex on the outside, set the bricks all around the top of wall, crosswise over the width of the blocks, and then fill the box up with sand to the bottom of the front row of bricks. Sink the potted herb plants in the sand deep enough so that sand spills over the top of the pot, thus hiding the pots completely and giving the illusion that the herbs grow in the sand itself.

Drench both the potted plants and the surrounding sand with

water. The sand, which remains moist for some time, even in hot weather, acts as a cooler for the plant roots.

Now, the plants: one plant each, in the 10-inch pots, of tarragon and mint; in the 6-inch pots, two of chives, two of garden thyme, two winter savory, two sweet marjoram or origanum, two basil, two rosemary, two lemon balm, one hyssop, one garden sage, and one each lovage and sweet cicely.

Sweet cicely, like lovage, does have a long taproot. Both these herbs do poorly in small pots *except* when the pots are sunk, as in this terrace box, in sand. In this situation, although they will not make anywhere near the growth they would in the garden, they grow well enough to supply the kitchen with snippings.

Plasticrete masonry blocks, which come in four different colors, red, green, goldenrod, and beige, are shaped to fit together to form a flower box. Several of these flower boxes can be arranged in a row, to form an easy-to-make, narrow terrace box.

## MAINTENANCE OF CONTAINER-GROWN PLANTS

The general rule, plant herbs in the garden in full sun, should be modified for herbs grown in movable containers, at least during hot spells in summer. Pots set on a stone or brick terrace bake in the glaring reflected heat of a midsummer day's sun. And even in the country, where the breeze is usually fresh, pots, tubs, and planter boxes dry out surprisingly fast. Therefore, if possible, arrange movable plants so that they are in the shade at least part of the day, particularly during long spells of hot weather. Set them against a wall, or under the edge of an awning, where shadows fall, part time.

In penthouse pot and box gardening, the gardener is faced with a major problem of drought. The gardener at the herb garden at the Cloisters in New York City told us that in this garden, situated as it is on a bluff above the Hudson River, she is obliged to combat what amounts to a real desert climate, so hot and dry are the city winds. A penthouse terrace offers a similar environment.

Herbs planted in a sizable, permanent terrace box—really a small garden in itself—are not quite as subject to drought conditions as are herbs in pots. But water both the terrace boxes and the plants in movable containers generously, at least once a day —more often if weather is extremely hot and dry or if plants are set *on* a wall.

If no water comes out of the drainage hole in a container, this is a red-flag warning that the hole is clogged, the water is backing up, and you will have a potful of mud, which is as bad for herbs as powder-dry soil. The remedy is to repot, making certain at the second potting that the drainage is adequate and properly laid.

After about a month, newly potted plants should have established a good root growth and it is time to begin feeding them at regular intervals. If you live in the country and have stable manure, make **Liquid Manure** and water it on, once a week.

Or use chemical plant food, the latter being preferable for indoor gardening, because it is less messy. Nearly all seed companies, farmers' supply houses, hardware stores, supermarkets, drugstores, and five-and-dime stores carry small bags of nationally advertised complete fertilizers such as Vigoro, Rapid-gro, and Plantabs, to mention a few.

The amount of artificial fertilizer to apply is usually about a teaspoon, dissolved in a gallon of water, watered on once a week. For assured results, read carefully and follow the directions on the package. The Hubbard-Hall Chemical Company recommends that one teaspoon of their plant food (50 per cent of the nitrogen organic) be dug into the soil of potted plants once a month, and we have found that this works well on potted herbs.

## POT-BOUND

There is no question that herbs deserve their reputation as spreaders and since, in a pot, there is not much room to spread, potted herbs must be repotted from time to time.

As an instance of what may happen to the roots of herbs in a container, mint is a good example. One day a plant of our spearmint, kept for a period of four months in a 12-inch ring pot, began to look poorly. There was no evident sign of disease. We had watered, and fed it liquid manure, regularly. Previously it had flourished. We lifted the plant from the pot and the trouble was apparent. This single plant, in less than half a year, had had, in a mint plant's fashion, a population explosion.

As previously noted, mint propagates itself by means of stolons (underground stems) which reach out from the mother plant, go down into the soil, and send up new plants, several inches away.

In the pot the stolons had multiplied and, looking for a way out, had circled around and around, growing ever longer, until finally they had filled the whole upper half of the container with a dense mass. Water could no longer penetrate and the core was powder-dry.

What to do with such a badly pot-bound plant? Root divide and repot. This means to pull apart the mass of stolons, leaving enough root growth on the mother plant to assure a good new start. Then divide the mother plant into three parts and replant only one of the divisions in the original pot. Fill thc pot, if possible, with entirely new soil. Old potting soil, particularly when artificial fertilizers are used, may contain residues not encouraging to plant growth. Throw the old soil onto the compost pile, where it can be mixed to good advantage with rotting organic matter.

Snip off the stems of the freshly potted plant to within 2 inches of the surface of the potting soil, water well, and keep in a shady spot until new leaves come.

As for the mass of leftover stolons, if you have no place to plant them outdoors, and can find no friend who yearns to grow mint, throw them away, but this is a pity. Stolons are used by commercial growers for mint progagation. They must, however, be planted before they dry out. So cover them with moist soil, if you would keep them. To plant, just lay a stolon in a shallow trench, cover with soil, and water regularly until a little new mint plant breaks ground.

The increase of tarragon in a pot environment is not as great as that of mint, but for best results, tarragon should be repotted at least after six months' time. By then the plant should be divided into three parts.

Origanum is another lusty grower. In fact it is safe to say that, for optimum results, redo your pots, planter boxes, and tubs of herbs at the end of four to six months, which means that most culinary herbs raised in containers are ready for division at the end of summer. If you want to winter over, but not use potted plants until the following spring, see Chapter 10. If you want to bring potted herbs into the house for winter use, read on.

## ESPECIALLY FOR THE INDOOR GARDENER

Much of what has been said so far on growing herbs in containers applies to the summer gardener who has a place outdoors on a terrace or flight of steps, under an awning, on a porch, or where you may. But the country dweller who has a sun "parlor" or a sunny kitchen window may grow a selection of fresh herbs indoors in winter to flavor dishes to tempt finicky appetites, come December, January, February, March, and April; and the city dweller may raise some potted herbs all year round.

The problems of growing herbs indoors are the same as those that beset gardeners who raise ornamental house plants. The best tool for this kind of gardening is a very green thumb.

From our own personal experience, over a period of years, we have found that most of the herbs we have suggested for an outdoor garden of herbs in pots do spendidly indoors, provided that the room in which they are placed receives some sun part of the day, and that the room is *cool*. Tender plants, such as myrtle and lemon verbena, are excluded from this cool treatment.

In fact we have successfully kept a long list of herbs, in our zero and below-zero climate, all winter long in our Resolite room, which has no heat at all. The room is so called, not from any resolution on our part, but because the roof is made of that relatively new building material, a translucent paneling, sold under several trade names, one of which is Resolite. The Resolite room, intended as a potting shed, is protected. It faces south, and two sides are walled with window glass which admit direct sun-rays.

The following herbs, set in pots on the stone and dirt floor in this room, have wintered over: garden and carpeting thyme, winter savory, hyssop, lemon balm, garden sage, costmary, mint, and origanum, but not sweet marjoram and not rosemary. Tarragon survived, but not in good condition.

It should be stressed, however, that herbs kept in such cold storage make little growth during the cold months. It is merely a means of wintering them.

A person who has an alcove sunroom which receives limited heat—say, up to 65 degrees maximum in the daytime and no lower than 40 degrees at night—has the optimum location for growing herbs in the house. In such a room all the herbs mentioned above, plus tarragon and rosemary, grow well.

In warmer rooms, or in the summertime indoors, compensate for greater heat by giving the herbs as much humidity as possible. Sprinkle the leaves, as well as the soil, with water. Obviously the indoor gardener must set his pots on plates or trays to keep water from seeping onto the floor or window sill. Aluminum pie plates, such as those in which frozen pies are sold, make good plates for small pots. A better arrangement is to set the potted plants on trays filled with 2 inches of gravel. Keep water in the trays, and set the plants close to each other, for plants give off moisture from their leaves, and all this helps to maintain the humidity so needed by plants in the house.

A special note on tarragon. Tarragon is an herbaceous perennial. Unlike thyme, which keeps its leaves all winter long, tarragon dies to the ground when a heavy frost strikes. A tarragon plant which is to be brought indoors for winter use should first be allowed to go through this natural rest period, though you may make the rest period short. Just leave the plant, if potted, on the porch or, if in the ground, on location, until a frosty night causes the stems to drop their leaves. Cut off the old stems, pot or repot, as the case may be—and don't forget, a pot for tarragon should be least 12 inches in diameter. Bring the potted plant indoors and it will think it is spring and sprout new stems.

A good selection of herbs for a window box in a kitchen window: rosemary, sweet marjoram, parsley, chives, garden sage, and garden thyme.

# 5. "AUX FINES HERBES"

Gather the herbs you grow in your garden. Bring a handful of fresh aromatic sprigs to the kitchen. The fragrance of the essential oils clings to your hands and permeates the air. A few moments later, the busy staccato sound of chopping is heard. The cook is preparing a recipe *aux fines herbes,* which simply means that he or she has stripped the leaves off the sprigs and is mincing them with a moon-bladed chopper in a wooden chopping bowl.

Minced fresh herbs are called for in many recipes, not alone in the classic French omelet. This is a practical way to add flavor to foods, for the cook can sprinkle *fines herbes,* like pepper and salt, on a roast of meat or fillet of fish, or mix a blend with other ingredients in an oven dish. To substitute dried herbs in the same recipe, see **Dried Herbs, Measure for Measure.**

First, a word on how to measure fresh chopped herbs. Just press the minced leaves gently down in the measuring spoon. Do not pack. A little practice and you will be able to judge how many sprigs to pick to make a teaspoonful—and by full we mean, as in all measurements, level, not heaping.

One species of herbs that is best reduced by snipping with a pair of herb scissors, rather than by chopping, is chives. The tubular leaves of chives tend to mash under the chopping blade.

For a recipe that calls for the classic *bouquet garni,* gather sprigs of the herbs listed, each about 4 inches long. Then, instead of chopping them, tie the sprigs together in a little bouquet, and about a half hour before the ingredients in the recipe are done, drop the herbs in the pot. Remove them before serving. A *bouquet garni* is used in liquid recipes, such as soups.

## FRESH HERBS FOR THE WINTER SEASON

The renaissance of herb growing in America makes it increasingly possible for the cook without a garden to buy certain kinds of herbs fresh—notably tarragon, dill, and fennel—in gourmet markets all year round. However, the average market often carries no fresh herbs, except, of course, the universal parsley. The answer to the problem of a fresh herb supply, then, for the herb grower in winter is the **Planter Box** and/or the freezer.

Frozen herbs retain their fresh color and flavor, and they are easy to process. To freeze herbs you will need:

polyethylene bags, 5½ by 3 inches
rubber bands
1 medium-sized wire strainer, or a wire lettuce basket
2 pans, large enough to submerge the lower half of the strainer
freezer marking pencil
watch or clock with a "second" hand
paper toweling

Select herbs that are in their prime. The leaves should be mature, lush, and green (or gray, as the case may be), with no sign of browning. Most herbs will be ripe for the freezer when just coming into bud.

Snip off sprigs about 4 inches long. Then fill one pan with cold water and chill by adding a dozen or so ice cubes. Set the second pan, three quarters' full of water, on the stove and let the water come to a boil.

Meanwhile mark the names of the herbs to be frozen on the freezer bags. (Some freezer pencils mark illegibly on wet bags.)

Caution: Freeze only one kind of herb at a time. Before freezing a second kind, renew the water, which will be impregnated with the flavor of the first herb. Dominant herbs such as lovage and sage will spoil the flavor of more delicate herbs.

When the water on the stove has come to a rolling boil, place four herb sprigs in the strainer, lower it into the boiling water, and blanch for 40 seconds. Then quickly transfer the strainer to the pan of ice water. Leave it in the cold water just long enough to chill (a few seconds), remove the herbs, and blot off most of the water on a paper towel. Drop the sprigs into a freezer bag. Lay the bag flat on the table, rub the palm of your hand over the bag, forcing out all air possible. (Air dries frozen foods.) Seal by turning back the open end of the bag, and secure it tightly with a rubber band. Place immediately in the freezer.

The following herbs freeze satisfactorily this way:

tarragon
origanum
sweet marjoram
thyme
lovage
sage
hyssop
winter and summer savory
mint
dill
lemon balm

For basil, follow the same procedure as above for blanching—that is, blanch the basil leaves while still attached to the leaf stems, but strip them *after* chilling. The basil stems are too thick and tough to go into the little bags. If you strip off the leaves before blanching, the leaves tend to mat in the pan and become discolored.

## DRIED HERBS, MEASURE FOR MEASURE

Dried herbs, like dried fruit—apples, raisins, and prunes—retain the recognizable flavor of the fresh product, although neither herbs nor fruit taste quite the same. Gourmets prefer fresh herbs. They are more delicate in flavor and they are, shall we say, fresher? And recipes in this book are made for the cook who has a garden. This is a fresh herb platter.

However, for a person who has no access to a source of green herbs, fresh-picked or frozen, we recommend dried herbs, particularly those dried and pulverized, as an acceptable substitute for the fresh; and for the cook who comes home late from the office to prepare dinner, they are a boon, for they are ready to use.

A good general rule to follow, and one which applies to all recipes in this book, is to use half as much of the dried, pulverized herbs as of the fresh, chopped herbs. The reason for this is that dried herbs are concentrated. For example, a tablespoon of fresh origanum or parsley, chopped fine and spread out on a tray to dry, shrinks to about half the fresh bulk, and if dried in the natural way, without artificial heat, much of the full flavor remains. Therefore, when a recipe calls for 1 teaspoon of fresh herbs chopped fine, substitute ½ teaspoon of the dried, pulverized herbs.

To test this rule, simply fill 2 cups with tomato juice. Into the first cup, mix ½ teaspoon of fresh chopped basil, and into the second, ¼ teaspoon of the dried product. Then taste.

There are some good dried herbs on the market, and some very poor ones. One problem with commercial dried herbs is that while some kinds, such as mint, retain their fresh flavor for a year, perhaps longer, others lose their strength within six months. Two herbs that, after a year in the dried state, taste the way we think hay must taste to anyone but a horse are parsley and chervil. Basil can be used, but certainly is not at its best, at the end of twelve months. Therefore, to forestall getting flavorless, dusty-tasting products, buy commercially dried herbs from a grocer who has a quick turnover of herb products.

A second problem with commercially dried herbs is that many of them are cured with artificial heat. To select the best, observe the color. The fresher the color, the better the product.

The ready cook will of course have on hand an assortment of seasonings to supplement the herbs. The following are indispensable.

**Seasonings**

Hungarian paprika
peppercorns
mustard seed
mustard flour (dry mustard)
cloves
ginger
cayenne pepper
tumeric
anise seeds
caraway seeds

The last two named are biennial herbs, easily raised, but the harvest of seeds comes in the second year, and for the busy gardener, it makes sense to buy these two kinds of seeds at the grocery store.

**Sauces**

soya
Worcestershire

**Thickeners** (in addition to white flour)

cornstarch
potato flour

Potato flour is superior as a thickener, even to cornstarch. Though not found in most American markets, it is usually stocked by Scandinavian stores, and those which carry a full line of Scandinavian foods.

Every cook has her own list of indispensable utensils, without which she feels that she cannot cook. Here are our favorites that never gather dust.

**OF POTS**

cast-iron Dutch oven, 10 inches in diameter; lower half, 3 inches, the interlocking lid, 2 inches deep; used frequently as two separate frying pans

enameled cast-iron cocotte, with cover, 10½ inches in diameter, 4¾ inches deep; for braising, making ragouts, etc.

an assortment of different-sized, round, oval, and oblong, come-to-the-table, earthenware casseroles

## FOR CUTTING AND SNIPPING, CHOPPING AND GRINDING

moon-bladed chopper, with wooden handle, and companion wooden chopping bowl

Vite Frite* a French hand press, with ten attachments:
- cutter for making julienne or shoestring
- cutter for making wedges
- cutter for making French-fries
- dicer
- double-edged slicer, one side for shredding, the other for scalloping
- ricer
- grater
- 2 strainers
- fruit squeezer

pepper grinder
coarse-salt shaker
French garden scissors
common meat grinder

Because the sturdy metal Vite Frite sets its four feet firmly on the table, the cook is less likely to cut a finger when dicing and

* May be purchased at Bazar Française, 666 Sixth Avenue, New York City.

slicing than when using the common kind of hand utensil. The Vite Frite is a wonderful aid in preparing apples for a stuffing, for making escalloped potatoes, and for doing much of the scullery work that precedes the creative part of cooking.

## FOR MEASURING, STIRRING, BEATING, AND BRUSHING

2 sets measuring spoons, one for dry, one for liquid
3 measuring cups, one for dry, one for liquid, and an extra
wooden stirring spoon
wire whisk
barbecue brush
electric mixer

## MISCELLANEOUS

lettuce basket
deep-well cooker (comes with some electric stoves, cooks vegetables without addition of water)

## COOKING WITH WINE

In early-American country kitchens, herbs and wine went hand in hand. Herbs were dried and vinegars steeped. Dandelion, cowslip, and elderberry wines were also homemade, as a matter of course. Winemaking was then no more unusual than making jelly. Blackberry brandy was a household word. The fancy sillabub, the base of which is wine or cider and milk, was taken to the cow and the milk was added with an expert squirt, direct from the udder, to give a natural froth.

Although the making of wine in the home does not seem to be in for a revival, wines are again finding deserved popularity in home cooking, and the combined use of herbs and wine brings nectar to an otherwise plain recipe.

Few people can afford to use costly vintage wines in the kitchen, but good *vin ordinaire* will do, and to reduce the expense, buy American wines in half or full gallon jugs.

If you choose but one bottle, make it sherry, the most universally popular wine for cooking.

For a three-bottle kitchen bar:

sherry
a white wine—Rhine, Riesling, or sauterne
a red wine—zinfandel or claret

For a more complete kitchen bar, a half gallon each:

sherry
Rhine wine
sauterne
zinfandel
burgundy

A fifth each of:

cognac or other grape brandy
Madeira wine

Sherry, an apéritif wine, is fortified by the addition of brandy, and so is of higher alcoholic content than the table wines. Choose a pale dry, cocktail type of sherry, unless a recipe calls for a sweet wine. Then use the dark, amber, cream or sweet sherry.

The only sherry, of course, that is rightly called sherry is imported from the vicinity of Jerez, Spain, but American vintners have named their sherries and most of their other wines after their prototypes in Europe.

There is some justification for the use of the name "sherry" among the California vintners, for many of them are direct descendants of settlers who came to this country from Spain, bringing with them the knowledge of the Old World producers, and cuttings of the most famous of the sherry grapes, the palomino.

Other California wines are made from other varieties of the Old World grape, *Vitis vinifera,* the grape that Noah planted in his vineyard and from which he made the wine he drank.

One red California wine, zinfandel, though, is American in origin, or rather confusion of origin. It comes from a grape of an unknown variety, the first cuttings having been imported from the Old World over a century ago by a Hungarian. Apparently unable to read the label on the cuttings, the Hungarian copied it as zinfandel. Zinfandel is a quite dry and tart red wine, very good for cooking. Rhine wine is its counterpart in a white wine. Burgundy is a rich, full-bodied red wine. The true sauterne is a semisweet wine, although some American sauterne types are dry.

We find that the pale dry cocktail sherry and the table wines mentioned, under the Gallo, the Petri, and the Guild labels, are all good cooking wines. Almadén Mountain Red is an excellent burgundy. All the wines from Napa Valley, California, are good, though usually quite expensive. There are many other good American brands, however, so choose your own favorite.

For the Madeira, a fortified wine, like sherry, buy the imported. It is expensive, but very little Madeira type of wine is produced in America, and this is a blend of sherries, or angelica and sherry.

The true cognac is brandy made from wine produced in the district of Cognac, in France, and nowhere else, but there are several good and less expensive grape brandies which do well for the kitchen bar. Try the Christian Brothers brandy, produced in Fresno County, California; or, if you prefer, the inexpensive brandy imported from France and bottled by Julius Wile Sons.

While we are on the subject of wines for the cook, sparkling as well as the still wines are used in special recipes, and we use champagne in one of our dessert recipes. Interestingly enough, some of the finest American champagnes are made from the native American grapes, in the Finger Lakes region. A leading champagne grape in this area is the Catawba, and a century ago the New York State Great Western brand of champagne was marketed under the name of Sparkling Catawba, and so it would probably be named today, if a prominent Bostonian horticulturist, Marshall P. Wilder, had not sampled the wine. Like others then living on the Eastern Seaboard, he referred to land across the Hudson River as "out West," and it was he who suggested that the company change the name from Sparkling Catawba to its present name, Great Western Champagne. This excellent sparkling wine is made from Catawba grapes, blended with Delaware, Dutchess, Isabella, and one or two other varieties, all American in origin.

An excellent California champagne, Almadén California Brut, is fermented from the Pinot Chardonnay, the Pinot Noir, and the Pinot Blanc or Sauvignon grapes, the same grapes that are used for the production of the champagnes of Europe. The brut is the driest of the champagnes.

## MISCELLANEOUS

Before you traipse out into the garden to gather those wonderful, sugary first fruits of your digging and hoeing, a last word of general advice to the cook. The old adage, the proof of the pudding is in the eating, is a maxim that a good cook need not be reminded of. Measure, yes—use the measuring spoons and cups meticulously in following a recipe—but variables in ingredients are inevitable. Your vegetables may be bigger or smaller than our vegetables; a roast of meat has more or less fat; seasonings vary in strength; and so do not neglect the measuring spoons, but, at the same time, do not neglect to taste, taste, taste.

Note that cooks have long misused the word "boil." An engineer we know once almost boiled himself when we tried to tell him that a slow "boil" was different from a fast rolling boil. He claimed that boiling was boiling, and he is quite right. Boiling is the point at which water reaches 212 degrees Fahrenheit. Boiled ham is usually cooked at a much lower temperature than actual boiling. The word to use for this, of course, is "simmer," at which heat bubbles slowly rise to the surface, and the water temperature is then only 180 degrees Fahrenheit. A few foods, such as spaghetti, are actually best cooked at a real boil.

## IMPORTANT REMINDER

Measure fresh herbs *after* chopping; and all measurements are level, not heaping. To substitute dried herbs for the fresh which are called for in recipes in this book, use half as much of the dried as of the fresh.

For economy, oleomargarine may be substituted for butter.

# 6. BRING OUT THE SALAD BOWL AND THE VEGETABLE POT

One of the enjoyable results of raising your own herbs is to have the home-grown ingredients for making herb vinegars, for use in salads and other dishes.

## VINEGAR DON'TS

The list of utensils *not* to be used in making vinegars is more important than things to be used. Don't use an aluminum pot to steep your vinegar in; don't use an aluminum funnel; and don't use metal caps for the bottles. They corrode. Don't use cider or grain vinegar, except for an occasional special recipe.

Now the "dos." Make it wine vinegar—red for garlic, white for tarragon, your own choice for other herbs. Steep the herbs in the vinegar in any covered crock of stoneware, earthenware, glass, or china that is large enough. Uncovered crocks invite fruit flies. Use a glass funnel for filtering, a wooden spoon to stir, and plastic caps, or corks, for bottle stoppers.

You can, of course, make a small amount of vinegar in a Mason jar. The following recipes, one a single-herb, the other a mixed-herb vinegar, will make enough to bring glamour to your salads all winter through, with some extra to give to a bazaar, or for Christmas presents.

After experimenting with these, try your own combinations of herbs, and let taste be your guide.

## BASIL VINEGAR

7 quarts basil leaves and buds
2 gallons white-wine vinegar

Harvest the basil when the plants are mature, about 20–24 inches high, and in fresh green leaf, with the flower buds just forming. If you have waited until the plants are in full blossom and are starting to fade, hurry, hurry, for the basil will soon be past its prime.

Cut the stems about 1½ inches from the ground, wash if necessary, and drip-dry. Strip off the leaves and buds and discard the hard main woody stems. To measure, just drop the leaves and buds into a quart container and press lightly down. Do not pack.

Put basil into the crock, pour on the vinegar, stir well with a wooden spoon, mashing the leaves against the sides of the crock. Replace cover.

Every other day, stir and crush the leaves, always with a wooden spoon.

When the flavor of the essential oil in the basil has become well infused into the vinegar (in about three weeks, perhaps longer—tasting will tell), strain through cheesecloth. Pack a few of the pickled leaves in a Mason jar for use in a sauce or dressing that calls for vinegar. Discard the remainder of the leaves.

Fold filter paper in a cone shape, place paper in a glass funnel, set the funnel in a pitcher or other container with a narrow enough mouth to hold the funnel upright.

To assure a sparkling clear product, filter twice. Then bottle. Before capping or corking the bottles, place a sprig of fresh green basil in each, for effect.

Makes a little over 14 pints.

## A MIXED-HERB VINEGAR

A specialty of our house.

- 3 cups minced basil leaves
- 1⅓ cups finely cut up chives
- ⅓ cup minced tarragon leaves
- ⅔ cup minced borage leaves
- ½ cup minced lemon-balm leaves
- ⅓ cup minced salad-burnet leaves
- ⅓ cup chopped garlic
- 1 cup chopped shallots
- 2 gallons red-wine vinegar

Start this mixed-herb vinegar when the basil is coming into bud. By then the other herbs listed should also be ready to harvest.

Gather the leaf herbs, wash if necessary, drip-dry. Then strip off the leaves and mince them.

Put the leaves with the garlic and shallots in a covered crock with the vinegar. Stir with wooden spoon, at least every other day.

When the essential oils in the herbs have become infused in the vinegar (in three weeks, maybe longer), then proceed as with **Basil Vinegar:** strain, filter, and bottle.

A sprig of salad burnet in each bottle adds a decorative touch.

Makes about 14 pints.

The indispensable tarragon (estragon) vinegar is made the same way as basil. But harvest the tarragon when the plants reach full height. You need not wait for the tarragon to bud. Cut the stems 1½ inches from the ground. A second crop will come. Pull off all the tender stems with leaves attached, for the tender stems of tarragon, as well as the leaves, are good for making vinegar. Discard only the main hard stems.

Among other sweet herbs not mentioned in the above recipes, and commonly used for making vinegar, are the leaves of mint and both the leaves and seeds of dill.

More rarely, flowers of some plants such as rosemary, or the petals of roses, are used.

## CLOUDY VINEGAR

If you use a good brand of commercial wine vinegar (United States standard, 5 per cent acidity), your herb vinegar should remain clear. If, however, you obtain some homemade vinegar, you may have trouble. It may get muddy-looking, in which case, strain it and heat it on the stove, just to the boiling point. Filter and bottle in clean bottles. This pasteurization should stop the acetic fermentation which is causing the cloudiness.

## WHAT GOES WITH WHAT

It is a rare treat to make a salad with your own, newly steeped herb vinegars. First, out to the Garden Salad Bowl with a basket on your arm to pick a suitable selection of ingredients. Look about you, let your imagination play, but choose carefully. Teach your eye to translate the flavor to your mouth. Then combine and recombine the fresh sweet herbs and the lettuce and the salad vegetables growing in the oval plot.

Mint goes well with upland cress, costmary, and endive. Basil goes with tomatoes, of course, and Oakleaf lettuce and peppers.

Cucumbers have an affinity for all the lettuces and taste good in combination with radishes, for sharpness, rocket, for an unusual touch, and lemon balm and dill. Chives or scallions pep up bibb lettuce and bland corn salad; add a few burnet leaves, or a few young borage leaves, and basil.

Mix Imperial lettuce leaves with Ruby, for effect; add chives and basil, and garnish with Yellow Pear tomatoes and chunks of cucumbers. Break up cos lettuce, add ringed peppers, serve with Red Plum tomatoes, basil, and rocket.

Use escarole to lend a bittersweet taste to other, milder greens such as corn salad. Sliced radishes are good with this combination.

Chinese cabbage is delicious with chopped dill leaves; add lemon balm and sweet cicely.

Parsley will appear in many meat and fish salads, chopped fine, but also makes a pretty garnish to serve on the edge of a green salad bowl.

The leaves from a sprig of tarragon improve the flavor of almost any salad combination.

For a starter, pick:

2 leaves rocket
2 leaves upland cress
1 large leaf basil
leaves from a 4-inch sprig tarragon
6 scallions
chicory (Green Curled endive)
cos lettuce

Pick enough of the chicory and cos to fill nearly two individual salad bowls. Wash and drip lettuce in salad basket, then wipe off remaining water with a clean kitchen towel. Break lettuce into bite-size pieces.

Now, for a dressing, assemble the following for:

## SALAD DRESSING MADE AT THE TABLE

pepper grinder
coarse-salt shaker
a caster holding cruet of herb vinegar, cruet of olive oil, jar of mustard flour (dry mustard)
wooden salad bowl
wooden fork and spoon
one clove garlic or rocambole (unless herb vinegar is strongly flavored with garlic)

Mash and rub the garlic or rocambole clove onto the bowl. Strip leaves off rocket and cress from tough center stem and snip these leaves and the basil into small bits in the bowl. Strip and add the whole tarragon leaves.

Pull off any brown outer leaves from the white stalks of the scallions and cut off upper half of tops and discard. Cut up finely the remaining leaves and stalks.

Pour on enough olive oil to coat lettuce leaves thoroughly on all sides. Toss well, add 1 teaspoon herb vinegar, toss, and sprinkle on ¼ teaspoon dry mustard. Use the pepper grinder and the salt shaker lightly. Toss again and serve.

Serves 2.

Good cooks agree that ready-mixed salad dressings, in general, are inferior to those prepared at the same time as the salad itself. Here is a ready-mix, however, which you can make months ahead of time, and it will taste just as if you had made it while the salad was being tossed.

The secret lies in pre-mixing all the ingredients *except* the olive oil.

## A DO-IT-AHEAD-OF-TIME FRENCH HERB SALAD DRESSING

2¾ cups herb vinegar
1 cup mustard flour (dry mustard)
¼ cup paprika
3 tablespoons salt
¼ cup sugar
1 teaspoon black pepper
1 teaspoon powdered ginger
1 tablespoon soya sauce
olive oil

Mix together and bottle: vinegar, mustard, paprika, salt, sugar, pepper, ginger, and soya sauce.

Makes 3 cups.

When ready to serve, just coat the salad greens thoroughly with olive oil. Shake well the bottle of pre-mix, and add a little of it, about 1 teaspoon for a salad for two—more according to size of salad. Toss again and serve.

## SOUR-CREAM SALAD DRESSING

½ teaspoon mustard flour (dry mustard)
1 teaspoon herb vinegar
1 teaspoon sugar
½ teaspoon salt
½ teaspoon paprika
1 teaspoon sour cream
3 teaspoons olive oil

Mix the mustard,vinegar, sugar, salt, and the paprika with the sour cream. Finally blend in the olive oil, until the dressing is smooth.

Serves 2.

Serve with a green or vegetable salad.

## RUSSIAN HERB DRESSING

2 tablespoons minced green pepper
½ teaspoon minced shallots
2 tablespoons chili sauce
1 tablespoon mixed herb vinegar
1 teaspoon fresh, chopped basil leaves
½ teaspoon pepper
¼ teaspoon salt
olive oil

Mix green pepper, shallots, chili sauce, vinegar, basil, and pepper and salt. Coat leaves and other ingredients in salad with olive oil. Add the dressing, toss, and serve.

Serves 2.

*The following sample recipes from Our Country Journal indicate approximate amounts of pickings to take from The Garden Salad Bowl for green and other salads.*

## FRESH HERB SALAD NO. 1

1 frying pepper
handful any lettuce leaves
handful corn-salad leaves
1 medium orange tomato
1 teaspoon chives, cut up fine

Cut off end, remove seeds and pith from pepper, and dice. Wash, drip-dry, and break up lettuce leaves and corn salad. Slice tomato. Add the chives.

Serves 2.

Serve with **French Herb Salad Dressing.**

## FRESH HERB SALAD NO. 2

1 small head or ½ large head Imperial lettuce or 5 heads bibb lettuce
1 clove garlic or rocambole
2 leaves rocket
12 small radishes, red or white
2 medium tomatoes
4 scallions, sliced

Wash and prepare lettuce, as per previous recipe. Rub bowl with garlic or rocambole. Strip rocket from tough inner stem and snip into salad bowl, with the lettuce. Cut off stem and root ends of radishes and slice thinly. Cut off stem end of tomatoes and dice. Add scallions.

Serves 5.

Serve with **French Herb Salad Dressing.**

## RED AND GREEN SALAD

4 medium-sized tomatoes
1 bell pepper
olive oil
salt and pepper
1 teaspoon fresh, chopped basil leaves

Cut tomatoes into wedge-shaped pieces, the size of a lemon wedge. Arrange around the outer edge of a narrow serving platter.

Cut off top of pepper, remove seeds and pith, and slice in narrow rings, crosswise. Arrange the pepper rings down the center of the platter, between the tomatoes.

Coat the tomatoes and peppers lightly with olive oil. Sprinkle with salt and pepper and the basil.

Serves 4.

## AVOCADO SALAD

1 avocado
3 heads bibb lettuce
1 teaspoon finely cut up chives

Peel, remove seed from avocado, and cut fruit in thin slices, lengthwise. Pull apart leaves of bibb lettuce and lay in circle around avocado. Sprinkle on the chives.

Serves 3.

Serve with **Sour-cream Salad Dressing.**

## BACON AND CUCUMBER SALAD

A satisfying summer luncheon salad.

1 cucumber
6 slices round Canadian bacon
6 leaves upland cress
handful lettuce leaves
1 teaspoon fresh chopped dill leaves
2 teaspoons finely cut up chives
olive oil
⅛ teaspoon mustard flour (dry mustard)
1 teaspoon herb vinegar
paprika
salt and pepper

Peel cucumber, cut in half, and slice in long thin strips. Cut bacon in narrow strips and sauté until crisp. Strip leaves of cress off tough center stem. Shred lettuce leaves. Mix cucumber, lettuce, cress, dill, and chives together, and coat well with olive oil. Sprinkle with the mustard, vinegar, paprika, salt, and pepper. Then add the bacon while still hot.

Serves 2.

Serve with strawberry shortcake for dessert.

## PEPPERONI SALAD

A main-dish luncheon salad.

6 Yellow Pear or 4 Red Plum tomatoes
1 bell or 2 frying peppers
12 thin slices pepperoni sausage
Imperial lettuce
**French Herb Salad Dressing**
2 hard-boiled eggs, shelled and sliced

Halve the Yellow Pear, or quarter the red tomatoes. Remove stem and pith and seeds from pepper, and cut in thin strips. Cut up pepperoni slices into small pieces. Mix the tomatoes, the pepper, and the pepperoni in two individual salad bowls, half in each. Break up and add enough lettuce leaves to fill the bowls. Toss with **French Herb Salad Dressing,** and top with egg slices.

Serves 2.

## SOUR-CREAM POTATO SALAD

4 cups boiled, peeled, cubed potatoes
2 tablespoons olive oil
¾ cup sour cream
2 teaspoons tarragon vinegar
4 scallions, cut up fine
3 tablespoons parsley leaves
salt and pepper
paprika

It is best to use a waxy rather than a mealy potato for this recipe. Do not overcook, or potatoes will mash when mixed.

Blend olive oil, a little at a time, into sour cream. Add vinegar and stir well. Add scallions, parsley, potatoes, and salt and pepper to taste. Coat potatoes with sour-cream mixture. Sprinkle lightly with paprika.

Serves 8.

Serve with **Dessert Pancakes** and **Lingonberries.**

## CHICKEN SALAD

4 tablespoons olive oil
8 tablespoons sour cream
2 teaspoons tarragon vinegar
2 teaspoons finely cut up chives
2 teaspoons finely chopped fresh tarragon leaves
6 teaspoons finely chopped parsley leaves
salt and pepper
2 cups, cut up, cooked chicken
1 cup cooked Lima beans
1 cup cooked, cubed carrots
4 large lettuce leaves

Blend the olive oil with the sour cream. Add the vinegar, chives, tarragon, parsley, and salt and pepper to taste. Mix with the chicken, Lima beans, and carrots. Serve on lettuce leaves.

Serves 4.

*Make those cucumbers which suddenly, in midsummer, hang too many and too big on the cucumber trellises in The Garden Salad Bowl into pickles.*

## EVERYDAY CUCUMBER PICKLES

Icebox pickles.

- 2 large cucumbers
- 2 medium-sized onions
- ⅔ cup tarragon vinegar
- 1 teaspoon salt
- ¼ teaspoon pepper
- 4 tablespoons sugar
- 3 teaspoons fresh, chopped dill
- 2 teaspoons fresh, minced parsley
- 3 whole grape leaves

Peel the cucumbers and slice them thinly. Ring the onions. Set in a bowl, alternating cucumbers and onions in layers. Add vinegar, sprinkle with salt and pepper, the sugar, and the herbs. Top with grape leaves and weight down with a plate. Let marinate 2–3 hours. Keep in the refrigerator, for current use.

## CUCUMBER GINGER PICKLES

For keeping.

8 cups peeled, sliced cucumbers
4 cups peeled, sliced onions
½ cup salt
2 cups basil vinegar
1½ cups sugar
2 teaspoons curry
1 teaspoon ground allspice
6 minced rosemary leaves
2 teaspoons minced lemon-balm leaves
1 teaspoon black peppercorns
2 teaspoons mustard seed
2 teaspoons powdered ginger

Place cucumbers and onions in bowl with salt and add water to cover. Let marinate 2 hours. Drain and discard liquid.

Mix cucumbers and onions in kettle with vinegar, sugar, herbs, and spices. Let come to a boil. Pack hot pickles in Mason jars. To prevent jars from breaking, set them on a wooden table or breadboard, with a metal spoon in each.

Cover pickles with the juice, cap, and turn upside down to seal.

Makes 6 pint jars.

*Turning from The Garden Salad Bowl to the fruits of the Vegetable and Herb Garden, the* FLAVOR CHART *lists the herbs that have an affinity for two kinds of vegetables, namely beans and tomatoes. There was no room on the chart to suggest the best combinations for the other vegetables, but the following selected recipes indicate choice herbs to go with these.*

## squash Squash SQUASH

Midsummer finds the gardener in the Garden Salad Bowl with little surplus except cucumbers.

The gardener in the Vegetable and Herb Garden will save for winter storage such vegetables as carrots and beets, and/or freeze them. Few vegetables in this garden should bolt to seed and waste, except zucchini summer squash, which are too watery to freeze. We have purposely suggested only one hill of zucchini because they are so prolific.

Soon after the first little cucumber-size green squash has appeared and has been picked and appreciated, the two-hill zucchini grower will find himself with a problem of what to do when suddenly confronted with dozens of overgrown fruit that resemble great, green, sausage-shaped balloons. Gardeners feel guilty, as though they were taking food out of the mouths of starving people, if they let this surplus end up on the compost pile. What to do?

No use offering the big old summer squash to friends. Chances are that they have already been given surplus whoppers by other two-hill zucchini gardeners. Secretly load up the cars of unsuspecting weekenders going back to the city, and let their consciences be bothered if they can't eat all that you so generously stowed away on the back seat of their car. Even with only one hill of zucchini, the squash keep right on coming and coming. It helps to reduce the surplus by varying your zucchini recipes as follows.

## ZUCCHINI SQUASH SAUTÉED NO. 1

1 young zucchini squash (may be quite large, but pick it before the seeds enlarge)
flour
1 egg
3 tablespoons butter
1 teaspoon fresh, chopped thyme leaves
salt and pepper

Slice zucchini crosswise in thin slices. Do not peel. Place flour in a paper bag, add zucchini, and shake the bag. Break egg in bowl and beat with a fork. Dip zucchini slices in the egg. Then dredge on both sides with flour.

Place butter and thyme in a heavy iron skillet over high heat until butter is melted; reduce heat so that fat does not burn. Add enough zucchini slices to cover bottom of pan, and sauté until golden brown on one side. Sprinkle with salt and pepper to taste, turn, and sauté on the other side. Prick with fork from time to time, and when squash is both brown and soft, it is done.

## ZUCCHINI SQUASH SAUTÉED NO. 2

1 young zucchini squash
flour
1 egg
olive oil
salt and pepper
2 teaspoons finely chopped savory leaves

Slice zucchini and coat with flour and egg, as in recipe for **Zucchini Squash Sautéed No. 1.**

Coat a heavy iron skillet with olive oil and add enough slices of zucchini to cover bottom of pan. Sauté on one side until golden brown, sprinkle with salt and pepper to taste, and savory; turn and sauté on the reverse side until brown, and soft to the fork.

Do you want to please the men? Serve this recipe for luncheon with broiled bacon, maple syrup, and butter, in the manner of hot cakes. Yum.

*Now, what to do with the jumbos?*

## A RECIPE FOR OVERGROWN ZUCCHINI SQUASH

1 large zucchini
salt and pepper
3 skinless frankfurters (or 3 slices bacon)
½ teaspoon finely chopped mint leaves
½ teaspoon finely chopped savory leaves
bread crumbs
Parmesan cheese
2 teaspoons butter

Peel squash, remove seeds, and dice. Sprinkle with salt and pepper, and cook in the deep-well cooker without water for 1½ hours. Or cook in top of a double boiler, also without water, until done.

Place half of the cooked squash in a buttered casserole with its own juice. There should be plenty of natural zucchini juice.

Cut frankfurters in thin slices, crosswise. Arrange on top of the squash and add remaining squash. Sprinkle on the herbs, then the bread crumbs, and last the Parmesan cheese. Dab with the butter. Bake in a slow oven, 250°, for about 40 minutes.

For a variation on the above recipe, substitute bacon for the frankfurters. Cut each slice in half and broil in the oven until crisp, turning at least once. Drain bacon on paper towels, crumble, and add a layer in place of the franks.

Also try **Zucchini Squash** as a canapé.

## BAKED BUTTERNUT SQUASH

2 Butternut squash
1 teaspoon chopped thyme leaves
salt and pepper
⅛ pound butter

Quarter squash, or, if squash is very large, cut into five pieces. Remove seeds and place squash in a roasting pan. Sprinkle each section with a goodly pinch of thyme, coarse salt, and freshly ground pepper. Add to each a generous dab of butter.

Put water in pan. Start with 2 cups, and if pan dries out during cooking, add a little more water.

Bake in an oven preheated to 350°, until squash meat is soft.

Serve 1 piece to a person.

## BAKED ACORN SQUASH

2 acorn squash
1 green pepper
4 teaspoons butter
4 teaspoons sherry
2 teaspoons finely chopped basil leaves
½ teaspoon powdered ginger
salt and pepper

Cut squash in halves, remove seeds, and place squash in a pan with about ½ inch of water.

Cut off stem end of pepper, remove pith and seeds, and mince. Spoon pepper into the squash. Add 1 teaspoon butter and 1 teaspoon sherry to each half. Sprinkle with the basil, ginger, salt, and pepper, and bake in a 350° oven until done.

Serves 4.

## CROOKNECK SQUASH

2 cups cubed squash
½ teaspoon salt
⅛ teaspoon pepper
½ teaspoon finely chopped tarragon leaves
1 tablespoon butter

If squash are young, remove stem and blossom end and cube, but do not peel. But with old squash, peel and core before cubing.

Simmer in water, not quite to cover, with salt, pepper, and tarragon. When squash is tender, drain excess water, add butter, and mash.

Serves 2.

*The following recipes are for other vegetables in the Vegetable and Herb Garden, incorporating the sweet herbs raised side by side.*

## RUTABAGA

2 cups peeled, cubed rutabaga turnip
½ teaspoon salt
1 teaspoon sugar
½ teaspoon minced thyme leaves
4 teaspoons butter

Rutabagas vary in size. This recipe calls for about 1 turnip.

Combine all ingredients except butter in a saucepan. Do not quite cover with water. Cook over medium heat until turnip gets soft. It should not be necessary to drain the turnip, as all the water should be absorbed.

Add butter and mash well.

Serves 4.

## BUTTERED BEETS

6 medium-sized beets
6 shallot bulbs
½ teaspoon salt
⅛ teaspoon pepper
butter
4 crushed cloves
½ teaspoon finely chopped basil leaves
1 teaspoon herb vinegar

Cut off beet tops and taproot. Wash. Peel shallots, and boil beets and shallots in water to cover, with salt and pepper, until done. Reserve stock for **Beet Consommé.**

Peel and slice beets. Melt butter in saucepan, add shallots, cloves, basil, and the vinegar. Coat beets with this herb butter.

Serves 4.

## SAVORY CARROTS

10 young carrots
½ teaspoon salt
¼ teaspoon pepper
½ teaspoon finely chopped savory leaves
1 tablespoon butter
2 teaspoons honey
½ teaspoon basil vinegar

Wash and scrape carrots, and cut in half crosswise. Boil in water to cover, with salt, pepper and savory, until carrots are tender. Melt butter in a casserole, add honey and vinegar, and keep on low heat. Roll carrots in casserole until well coated with butter and honey.

Serves 4.

## SHALLOT BREAD

3 shallots, chopped fine
⅛ pound butter
1 loaf Italian-style bread

Mash shallots with the butter. Cut bread almost through, in serving-size slices. Spread the slices with the shallot butter. Wrap bread in heavy aluminum cooking foil and place in a 400° oven long enough to heat through.

## CHARD GREENS

1½ quarts chard leaves
½ teaspoon finely chopped summer savory
½ teaspoon salt
⅛ teaspoon pepper
1 hard-boiled egg, chopped fine

Cook chard leaves only (reserve stalks) in about 1 cup of water, with savory, salt, and pepper, until tender. Drain off excess water. Chop leaves and put them into a casserole. Sprinkle the egg on top.

Serves 4.

## CHARD STALKS BEURRE NOIR

6 chard stalks
salt
3 tablespoons butter
½ teaspoon finely chopped basil leaves
pepper
½ teaspoon lemon juice

Cut stalks in 4-inch lengths. Boil in water to cover, with salt, until tender.

Heat butter in skillet, stirring constantly until it starts to brown. Then blend basil, pepper, and lemon juice into butter. Remove from stove and pour *beurre noir* over the stalks.

## OKRA AUX ÉCHALOTES

2 cups okra pods, measured after slicing
¼ cup peeled, sliced shallots
1 Italian green frying pepper, minced
3 tablespoons butter
salt and pepper
1 teaspoon finely chopped fresh basil leaves
1 teaspoon finely chopped fresh parsley leaves
2 medium-sized tomatoes

Cut stem ends off okra, and slice crosswise, in ¼-inch pieces. Sauté shallots and the green pepper in 2 tablespoons butter, in a saucepan, until shallots are golden. Add okra, sprinkle with salt and pepper to taste, and sauté 3 minutes.

Grease a casserole with the remaining butter, turn okra and shallots into the casserole, and sprinkle on the herbs. Top with thinly sliced tomatoes. Sprinkle a little salt and pepper on the tomatoes. Bake about ½ hour in a 350° oven.

Serves 4.

## KOHLRABI EN CASSEROLE

1 whole fennel
2 cups peeled, sliced kohlrabi
3 tablespoons butter
1½ cups white sauce*
salt and pepper
grated Parmesan cheese
paprika

Strip outer stringy leaves off fennel and discard. Slice fennel thinly. Boil fennel and kohlrabi until tender. Grease a casserole with 1 tablespoon butter, mix in kohlrabi, fennel, white sauce,* salt, and ground black pepper, to taste. Sprinkle on grated cheese and decorate with lines of paprika.

Bake in a medium oven until brown on top, about ½ hour.

Serves 4.

*White sauce. Blend 2 tablespoons butter with 1½ tablespoons flour, in top of double boiler. Mix in slowly, with wire whisk, 1½ cups milk.

## CREAMED FENNEL AU VIN BLANC

1 whole fennel
¾ cup light cream
¼ cup white wine
2 tablespoons potato flour
2 tablespoons butter
½ teaspoon salt
¼ teaspoon ground pepper
½ teaspoon finely chopped savory leaves
½ teaspoon finely chopped thyme leaves

Cut stems off bulblike leaf base of fennel. Strip leaf base of stringy outer leaves. If stems are very young and tender, use them too.

Cut fennel into ¼-inch pieces and boil in water to cover, until tender, about 40 minutes. Set stock aside.

Place fennel in upper part of double boiler. Blend cream, wine, and potato flour. Add 1 cup of fennel stock. Pour over fennel.

Add butter and seasonings, and heat until butter has melted, and sauce has thickened.

Serves 4.

## SNAP-BEAN CASSEROLE

A hearty luncheon dish.

2½ cups snap beans, measured after cutting
½ teaspoon salt
1 tablespoon butter
1 teaspoon cornstarch
½ cup light cream
½ teaspoon finely chopped savory leaves
⅛ teaspoon pepper
1 egg
bread crumbs
sharp Cheddar cheese
3 strips lean bacon

This is a good recipe in which to use snap beans that are getting big.

Cut off ends and tips, slice crosswise in pieces about an inch long, and cook in water with salt until nearly done. Do not let beans get too soft. Reserve stock.

Grease a casserole with the butter and add beans. Blend cornstarch with cream, stir in ¼ cup bean stock, savory, and pepper, and beat in the egg with a fork. Pour this mixture into the bean casserole. Sprinkle lightly with bread crumbs, top with very thin slices of cheese, enough to make a layer over the beans. Cut bacon strips in halves crosswise and lay on top of cheese.

Bake in oven preheated to 400° until bacon is crisp.

Serves 4.

## GINGER BEANS

1½ quarts snap beans
salt

2½ tablespoons olive oil
1 tablespoon tarragon vinegar
1 teaspoon Rhine wine
½ teaspoon powdered ginger
1 teaspoon finely chopped tarragon leaves
pepper

Cut off ends of beans and, if very young and tender, leave whole. Otherwise French them, which simply means to slice them once or twice lengthwise.

Cook beans in saucepan with salted water to cover until done. Do not overcook.

Pour off water, coat the beans with olive oil, add vinegar, wine, ginger, and tarragon, and sprinkle lightly with pepper. Toss and warm through.

Serves 6.

NOTE: Serve young whole beans, prepared in this way, and chilled, as a canapé.

## RED CABBAGE

5 strips lean bacon, cut in small squares
1 cup shredded onions
2 pared, cored, and diced apples
2 pints shredded red cabbage
4 tablespoons butter
2 tablespoons mixed-herb vinegar
½ teaspoon caraway seeds
¼ teaspoon anise seeds
½ teaspoon finely chopped thyme leaves
½ teaspoon finely chopped spearmint leaves
6 cloves
2 teaspoons salt
3 teaspoons sugar
¼ teaspoon pepper

Sauté bacon until crisp, add onions, and sauté until transparent. Do not brown. Add apples and cook until soft.

Bring cabbage to a boil in 2 cups water. Add bacon and all other ingredients to cabbage. Boil until cabbage is tender.

## JULIENNE PEPPERS

3 frying or bell peppers
1 tablespoon olive oil
½ teaspoon fresh, chopped basil leaves
½ teaspoon cut up chives
¼ teaspoon salt
⅛ teaspoon pepper
2 tablespoons sauterne

Cut off stem ends of peppers, remove pith and seeds, and cut julienne style. Heat oil in frying pan, add peppers, and sprinkle on the herbs, salt and pepper. Sauté peppers until they begin to get soft.

Pour on sauterne, and sauté until peppers are done. If too dry, add more wine.

Serves 3.

## MANGE-TOUT PEAS

A recipe without an herb, believe it or not!

1 pint edible-podded peas
salt and pepper
butter

We often use a touch of fresh chopped mint leaves with common garden peas. We use nothing with the *mange touts* except salt, pepper, and butter. The taste of these delectable peas is so distinctive and unusual, we do not care to dominate or even modify it with any other flavor.

Be sure to pick the edible-podded peas as soon as the pods have attained their length and before the peas begin to swell. When peas make small bumps in the pods, let them mature. Then shell, and serve the peas as *petits pois.*

Boil the young pods in water, not quite to cover, with salt and pepper, until pods are tender. Drain water, and reserve. Stir a generous dab of butter in with peas.

Serves 2.

The water in which the peas were cooked makes an excellent vegetable stock for soup.

*The following recipes are for a few vegetables, such as potatoes, not included in the Vegetable and Herb Garden, and mushrooms, so good to serve sautéed and broiled, with all kinds of meat and fish, and the other fresh herb platters.*

**BASIL POTATOES**

2 pounds small white potatoes
2 teaspoons finely chopped basil leaves
3 tablespoons flour
1 egg
salt and pepper
3 tablespoons bread crumbs
1 tablespoon olive oil
2 tablespoons butter

You may buy small whole, peeled potatoes, already cooked, in 1-pound cans. If you use fresh potatoes, peel and parboil them. Do not overcook. They must be firm.

Place potatoes, basil, and flour in a paper bag and shake until potatoes are coated. Drop egg in bowl, beat with an electric mixer, and turn potatoes into the bowl. Coat potatoes with egg and sprinkle with salt and pepper to taste. Roll potatoes in bread crumbs. Heat olive oil and butter in skillet. Sauté potatoes until golden brown, turning often.

Serves 16, in these days of calorie counting.

## FENNEL POTATOES EN CASSEROLE

5 medium-sized potatoes
2 teaspoons finely chopped fennel leaves
4 tablespoons butter
⅓ cup milk
salt and pepper
1 egg
¼ cup milk
paprika

Boil the potatoes with their jackets on until they are well done. Peel, place in mixing bowl with the fennel, 3 tablespoons butter, ⅓ cup milk, salt and pepper to taste. Mash well, and turn into a greased casserole.

Beat the egg and ¼ cup milk with a fork, and spread over the top of the potatoes. Dot with the remaining butter, sprinkle with paprika, and bake in a 350° oven until the top is brown.

Serves 6.

## POTATOES AU GRATIN

3 cups boiled, peeled, cubed potatoes
1 tablespoon potato flour or cornstarch
1⅓ cups medium cream
⅛ teaspoon pepper
¼ teaspoon salt
bread crumbs

2 medium-sized tomatoes, sliced
½ teaspoon finely chopped basil leaves
butter

Place potatoes in a greased casserole. Blend potato flour or cornstarch into cream. Add pepper and salt and pour over the potatoes. Sprinkle generously with bread crumbs. Arrange tomato slices on top, sprinkle with basil, dot with butter, and bake until top is brown in an oven preheated to 350°.

Serves 6.

## POTATOES BAKED

6 baking potatoes
1 teaspoon finely chopped basil or lovage leaves
salt and pepper
butter

Core halfway through each potato with an apple corer. Remove core and set aside.

Blend herb leaves, salt, and pepper with butter, allowing about ½ teaspoon butter to each potato. Spoon butter into holes, replace cores, and bake until the potatoes are well done.

## SCALLOPED POTATOES

5 medium-sized potatoes
butter
salt and pepper
4 eggs
1 cup milk
1 teaspoon finely chopped chervil leaves
4 ounces Muenster or a similar cheese
paprika

Peel and boil potatoes and cut in thin slices. Arrange potatoes in a greased casserole, sprinkle with salt and pepper, layer for layer. Whisk the eggs with the milk, add chervil, and pour mixture over potatoes, mixing in thoroughly. Dice cheese and spread on top. Sprinkle with paprika, cook until brown on top and the eggs have jelled in an oven preheated to 350°.

Serves 6.

## CORN IN THE JACKET

You have not tasted corn on the cob until you do it this way. Count on 1 or 2 ears of corn per person.

2 ears corn, with husks on
¼ teaspoon salt
⅛ teaspoon pepper
¼ teaspoon fresh, chopped thyme leaves
2 teaspoons butter

Wrap each ear of corn, with husks on, in heavy aluminum cooking foil. Roast in coals for 20 minutes.

Blend salt and pepper and thyme into butter. Husk corn and serve with this herb butter.

The smoked-corn-and-herb flavor is a perfect combination.

## SAUTÉED ARTICHOKE HEARTS

1 teaspoon finely chopped tarragon leaves
1 teaspoon finely chopped parsley leaves
1 15-ounce can artichoke hearts
beef or lamb fat.

Sprinkle the herbs on the artichoke hearts and sauté them lightly in fat, turning constantly.

Serves 3.

## CAULIFLOWER CASSEROLE

1 large head cauliflower
salt
butter
1 teaspoon caraway seeds
2 teaspoons finely chopped tarragon leaves
2 teaspoons finely chopped savory leaves
1 cup milk
2 tablespoons cornstarch
1 cup cauliflower stock
pepper
bread crumbs
4 ounces cheese, common mild Cheddar
paprika

Remove greens from cauliflower and cut cauliflower into bite-size pieces. Boil in salted water, not quite to cover, in a covered pan until done, about 20 minutes. Underdo rather than cook too long, because the cauliflower is to be cooked again, in the casserole.

Arrange cauliflower in a buttered casserole and sprinkle on the caraway seeds, the tarragon, the savory, and the salt. Mix the milk and cornstarch and pour over cauliflower. Add stock and stir. Sprinkle with pepper and cover with bread crumbs.

Cut cheese in shape of French-fried potatoes, about 18 slices. Arrange cheese in wheel shape on top of cauliflower. Sprinkle with paprika, dot with butter, and bake in a preheated oven, starting at 400°. When liquid begins to simmer, reduce heat to 300°. Cook about 1 hour.

Serves 8.

## OF MUSHROOMS

Some people pick their own mushrooms, some grow their own, but most buy them at the market. For the latter, the price of mushrooms is important. At certain times of the year they are scarce and sell anywhere from eighty cents to a dollar a pound, or else you can't get fresh mushrooms at all. For those who must have mushrooms to complete a variety of menus, we recommend buying a basketful when the price is right, usually late fall or winter. Use what you need at the time, and dry the remainder of the caps.

## DRY YOUR OWN MUSHROOMS

Cut off the stems of common store mushrooms (*Agaricus campestris*), about ⅛ inch from the cap. Set aside stems. Wipe each cap with a damp paper towel. Wash the caps only if they are very dirty—in which case, spread out to dry thoroughly on paper towels. Do not peel the caps.

Thread a darning needle with strong white thread, knot the end of the thread around the center of a toothpick, and thread the caps, with the stem sides facing down. Hang the strings in a dry corner, until the mushrooms are dehydrated, and then bottle them in glass jars.

These dried mushrooms come in very handy for soups, ragouts, and gravies.

Now as to what to do with all those stems. Make them into **Mushroom-stem Canapé Piquant**, and freeze the canapé until wanted.

## BROILED MUSHROOM CAPS

1 pound mushrooms
butter
½ teaspoon finely chopped thyme leaves
salt
pepper

Cut stems from mushroom caps. Save stems for soup or gravy stock. Sauté the caps in frying pan, stem side down, in butter, for about a minute. Turn over, making sure that each cap is well coated with butter. Sprinkle with thyme, salt, and pepper. Then set pan under broiler, with mushrooms cap side up, and broil until caps are brown.

## SHERRY MUSHROOMS

1 pound mushrooms
⅛ pound butter
⅓ cup sherry
½ teaspoon cornstarch
½ teaspoon soya sauce
⅛ teaspoon finely chopped thyme leaves
½ teaspoon finely chopped sweet-marjoram leaves
salt and pepper

Cut mushroom stems from caps, and slice stems crosswise. Slice caps vertically. Melt butter in iron skillet and sauté mushrooms about 10 minutes over medium heat, turning and stirring constantly.

Mix sherry with cornstarch, add soya sauce and herbs, and stir into mushrooms. Let come to a boil. Sprinkle with salt and pepper to taste. When sauce thickens, remove immediately and turn into a casserole. Heat when ready to serve. Serve on toast.

Serves 6.

*The following two recipes are for the cook who likes to gather wild mushrooms, but common store mushrooms may be substituted for the wild.*

## SAUTÉED SHAGGY COPRINUS MUSHROOMS

2 cups Coprinus caps
2 tablespoons butter
2 tablespoons sherry
¼ teaspoon thyme
salt and pepper

The shaggy Coprinus mushroom (*Coprinus comatus*) grows commonly in pastures and along roadsides, mainly in late summer and autumn. It is a striking mushroom. The tall, cone-shaped, whitish cap is covered with yellowish scales, but it does not retain this pleasing form for long. Within a short time after the cap pushes through the surface of the ground, often in a matter of hours, the cap expands, the gills deliquesce, and the whole cap sinks into a blackish inky mass, which gives to this, and other species of Coprinus, the common name of "inky."

The Coprinus *must* be picked young, while the cap is still firm and cone-shaped, and before the ink forms. Then it has a delicate and delicious flavor. In fact it is classed by some mycologists as one of the best edible mushrooms. And none of the writers on mushrooms whose works we have read reports any of the Coprini to be poisonous, a comforting thought for the truly amateur mycologist who gathers a species new to him with trembling fingers, lest he mistake it for the dreaded poisonous fungi. With a good picture and a simple description from a mushroom book, the shaggy Coprinus is easy to identify.

To return to the recipe, to prepare Coprinus for cooking, cut stems off level with bottom of the cap and discard stems. While it is usually unnecessary to wash most mushrooms, it is nearly always necessary to wash the Coprinus because so much earth sticks to the caps. To dry them, roll them in paper towels, and squeeze them gently to get rid of excess water.

Split caps lengthwise, in halves. Melt butter in iron skillet, and when the pan is hot, add mushrooms. Sauté them, turning mushrooms frequently. When mushrooms start browning, pour on sherry and add thyme, salt, and pepper. Cook about 2 minutes more, stirring them gently. Serve on toast.

Serves 6.

## PICKLED SHAGGY COPRINUS MUSHROOMS

2½ cups young Coprinus mushroom caps
2 cups basil vinegar
1 cup sugar
1 tablespoon sherry
¼ teaspoon finely chopped thyme leaves
½ teaspoon black pepper
few grains cayenne pepper
1 teaspoon ginger
salt to taste

To prepare the Coprinus, see recipe above.

Bring vinegar to a boil in a saucepan. Mix all the ingredients, except the mushrooms, with the vinegar. Boil another minute. Add mushrooms and boil 5 minutes more. Then bottle the mushrooms while hot, cover with the juice, and seal.

Makes 1 pint.

# 7. TO BRAISE, TO BROIL, TO ROAST AND STEW

The herb **Flavor Chart** gives the cook a general idea of which herbs go best with beef, veal, lamb, pork, and poultry, and this is for use in recipes in your own recipe file. The meat recipes that follow list specific herbs and give specific measurements. Remember, if you use dried herbs, substitute half the amount of the dried for the fresh herbs called for in these recipes.

Now, to order the meat. Count on half a pound, bone in, per person, and a quarter pound of boneless. There is some disagreement among cooks as to whether frozen meat is as good as unfrozen. But on one question almost everyone agrees. With the exception of pork, the meat should be hung in the cooler room in a locker at a temperature of thirty-four degrees before it is eaten, or put in the freezer.

Real beef lovers insist that beef be hung three weeks. Five days is sufficient for lamb. Some people leave chickens in the cooler room only forty-eight hours, while others prefer a period of five days.

After meat has been properly hung, we like the frozen as well as we do the unfrozen, with two exceptions. Frozen meat is certainly convenient, because it can be kept for months without fear of spoilage, and it gives the cook a wonderful opportunity to lay in a supply when the price is low. However, frozen hamburger or any other frozen ground meat is not nearly so good as the fresh ground, because after it has thawed, it gets too watery. And smoked and salted meats lose something of the quality of those kept merely refrigerated. These include bacon, ham, and smoked turkey. But when one receives a present of a jumbo smoked ham or turkey which cannot be consumed all at one sitting, the freezer is of course the answer.

Americans are traditionally beefeaters, and so we start our meat recipes with beef. The man of the family, generally the master of the brazier, approaches the charcoal grill with a ritualistic fervor. No one can tell him how to broil a steak. He has his own way, which in most instances consists simply of broiling the meat and shaking on the pepper and salt. The only question is, how long to broil, how much to let the fat flame, and when to douse the coals.

We venture, therefore—somewhat uneasily, but with enthusiasm—to offer as the first beef recipe a variation on this broil-it -and -don't -add -anything -to -the -sirloin -porterhouse -except -a -parsley -garnish theme. The following recipe calls for a steak barbecue sauce.

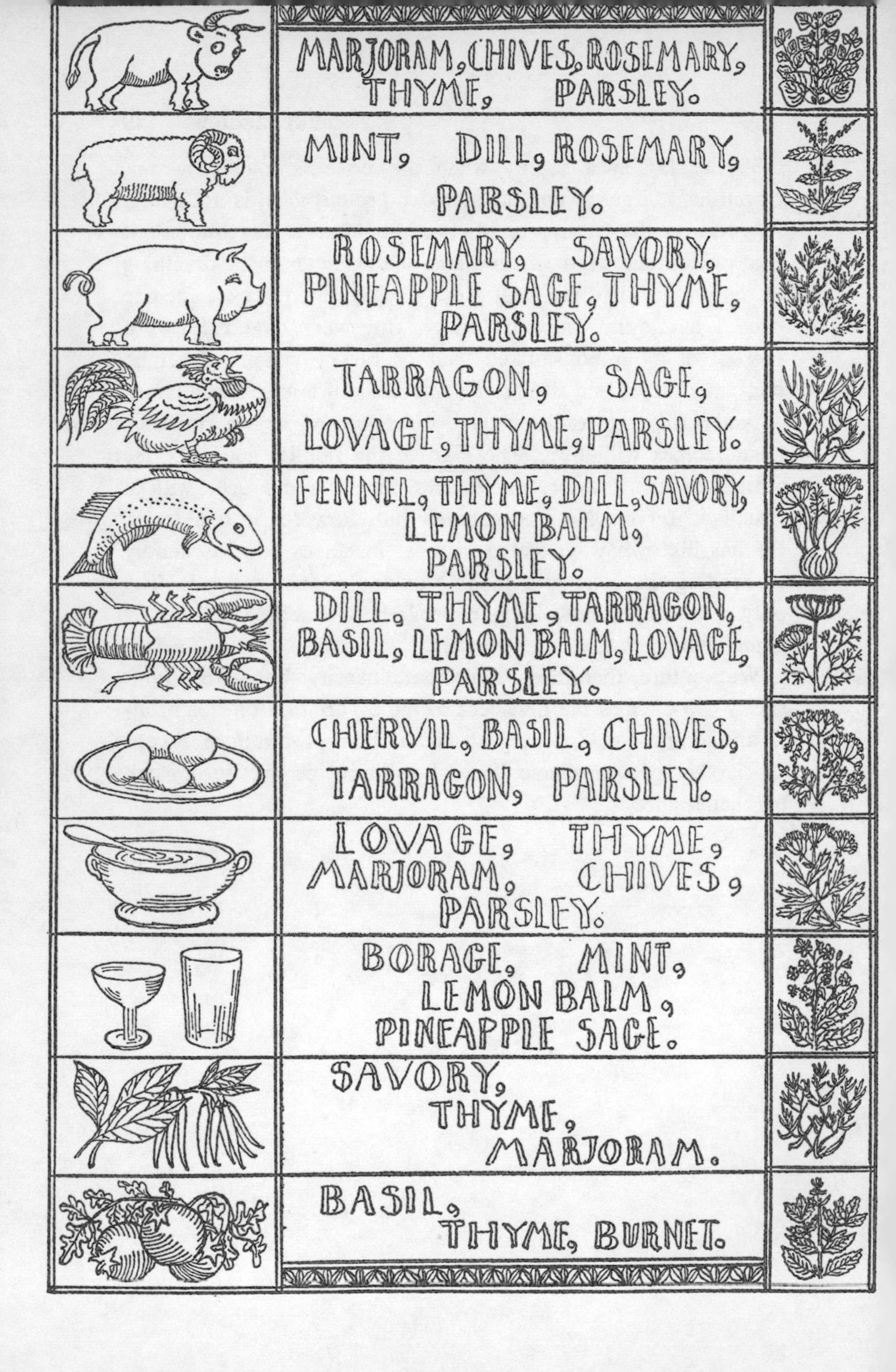
MARJORAM, CHIVES, ROSEMARY, THYME, PARSLEY.
MINT, DILL, ROSEMARY, PARSLEY.
ROSEMARY, SAVORY, PINEAPPLE SAGE, THYME, PARSLEY.
TARRAGON, SAGE, LOVAGE, THYME, PARSLEY.
FENNEL, THYME, DILL, SAVORY, LEMON BALM, PARSLEY.
DILL, THYME, TARRAGON, BASIL, LEMON BALM, LOVAGE, PARSLEY.
CHERVIL, BASIL, CHIVES, TARRAGON, PARSLEY.
LOVAGE, THYME, MARJORAM, CHIVES, PARSLEY.
BORAGE, MINT, LEMON BALM, PINEAPPLE SAGE.
SAVORY, THYME, MARJORAM.
BASIL, THYME, BURNET.

## PORTERHOUSE STEAK OVER THE COALS

1 tablespoon olive oil
1 teaspoon tarragon vinegar
2 tablespoons white wine
1 tablespoon bourbon whisky
½ teaspoon finely chopped sweet marjoram leaves
1 shallot, minced
1 faggot rosemary, 6 sprigs, each about 6 inches long
briquettes or charcoal
1 3-pound porterhouse steak
salt and pepper

Mix the olive oil, vinegar, white wine, bourbon, sweet marjoram, and the shallot, and let this barbecue sauce marinate in the refrigerator at least an hour. Start the briquettes with lighting fluid about 20 minutes before you broil the steak. If charcoal is used, start the fire later, as charcoal ignites more quickly. When the coals give off an even glow, clamp the steak in a long-handled grill. Throw the rosemary faggot on the coals and start broiling the steak immediately, while the rosemary is smoking.

Broil on one side for 10 minutes and brush with the sauce. Turn and broil on the reverse side for 10 minutes and brush this side with sauce. Then broil on fatty ends until the fat gets crisp. Place steak on platter and pour on remaining sauce. Sprinkle with salt and pepper. This makes medium-rare meat.

Serves 6.

Serve with **Corn in the Jacket, Potatoes Baked, Shallot Bread,** and **Fresh Herb Salad No. 2.**

---

FLAVOR CHART

The herbs named in each block are suggested for the foodstuff illustrated on the left. The herbs sketched on the right we have found most sympathetic—viz., from top to bottom: beef – marjoram, lamb – mint, pork – rosemary, fowl – tarragon, fish – fennel, shellfish – dill, eggs – chervil, soup – lovage, drinks – borage, beans – savory, tomatoes – basil.

## BOEUF ROULADE

This recipe makes a change from the usual ground-beef cycle of meat balls, meat loaf, etc. It goes well with smörgåsbord, as a substitute for the customary meat balls.

2 eggs
4 slices bread
2¼ pounds ground chuck
¾ cup chives, cut up fine
1½ teaspoons finely chopped origanum leaves
¼ cup finely chopped parsley leaves
1 teaspoon finely chopped lovage leaves
1 teaspoon powdered ginger
1 teaspoon salt
½ teaspoon pepper
capers
5 Italian green sweet peppers
butter

Break eggs into a bowl. Crumble the bread into the eggs and add the meat, herbs, ginger, salt, and pepper. Knead thoroughly, then pat the mixture into flat patties about 4 inches square. Stick 10 capers onto each patty. Remove seeds and pith from peppers and slice into narrow strips. Place five strips of green pepper in the center of each patty, fold the patty over the peppers, and pat into a roll. Make sure the pepper strips are completely sealed in.

Set two well-buttered skillets on the stove over high heat. When the butter begins to sizzle, roll the patties into the skillets, so that each one gets buttered all over. Sauté until brown, turning them constantly, to brown them equally on all sides. Turn them into a casserole.

Serve with a simple brown gravy as follows.

1 bouillon cube
1 teaspoon soya sauce
drippings from both skillets
1 teaspoon sugar
3 teaspoons flour
¼ cup thin cream
½ cup milk

Dissolve the bouillon cube in the soya sauce. Combine the drippings in one skillet and place on the stove over high heat. Brown the sugar in the drippings, stirring rapidly to prevent burning. When brown, add flour, and let flour brown, continuing to stir. Add soya sauce. Pour in cream and milk, stirring constantly and scraping the bottom of the pan to prevent sticking. When gravy begins to thicken, pour it over the meat. Cover the casserole and bake in a 350° oven for ½ hour.

Makes 16 patties; serves 8.

Serve with **Red Cabbage, Basil Potatoes,** and **Avocado Salad.**

## BEEF AND MUSHROOM RAGOUT

1 cup shallots
1 pound mushrooms, medium to large caps
olive oil
butter
1¼ pounds boneless beef stewing meat, cut in 1-inch cubes
5 radishes, sliced
1 tablespoon mustard seeds
1 bay leaf
½ teaspoon finely chopped hyssop leaves

⅛ teaspoon finely chopped sage leaves
½ teaspoon black peppercorns
1 teaspoon powdered ginger
2 cups cubed carrots
2 medium-sized potatoes, diced
½ cup red wine
salt and pepper
paprika

Take outer brown leaves off shallots and leave whole.

Cut stems of mushrooms into small pieces and set caps aside.

Cover bottom of skillet lightly with olive oil. When hot, add ⅛ pound of butter and brown the meat. Add mushroom stems, shallots, radishes, and seasonings to skillet. When shallots start to get soft, add enough water to cover ingredients. Remove from top of stove. Put lid on skillet, and place in preheated, 375° oven for about ½ hour, or until the meat is tender. Then add the carrots and potatoes, and when these are done, pour on the wine and turn ingredients into a buttered casserole.

Now sauté mushroom caps in butter and sprinkle them with salt and pepper to taste. Top the casserole dish with the mushroom caps and sprinkle with paprika. Keep in warm oven until ready to serve.

Serves 8.

Serve with **Fresh Herb Salad No. 2.**

## BEEF TONGUE AU VIN BLANC

1 smoked beef tongue
cloves
2 tablespoons sugar
1 teaspoon ginger
1 teaspoon mustard flour (dry mustard)
1½ cups white wine
2 medium onions, ringed
1 tablespoon capers
12 plums, cut in halves and pitted
1 banana, peeled and cut lengthwise in thin strips
1 teaspoon finely chopped sweet-cicely leaves
1 teaspoon finely chopped basil leaves

Boil tongue until tender (2–3 hours). Discard stock, because it is too salty. Skin tongue, remove roots and fat, and stick with cloves. Place on side in heavy iron skillet, and sprinkle with 1 tablespoon sugar, the ginger and mustard. Add wine, onions, capers, and plums to the skillet. Arrange strips of banana on tongue. Sprinkle the other tablespoon of sugar on the banana and add chopped herbs to the skillet.

Place the uncovered skillet in an oven preheated to 350°. Roast about ½ hour, or until top is brown, basting every 10 minutes.

Serve with **Buttered Beets, Chard Stalks Buerre Noir, Fresh Herb Salad No. 1,** with **Champagne Compote** for dessert.

## ROAST BREAST OF VEAL

1 4½–5 pound breast of veal
1 clove garlic
salt
flour
pepper
1 teaspoon chopped rosemary leaves
1 teaspoon ground lovage leaves
¼ cup olive oil
fatty salt pork
1 cup water
⅓ cup Rhine wine
1 teaspoon capers

Make certain that the veal is good before buying it. Veal meat should be nearly white, with just a tinge of pink. Poorly fattened calves, or those too old to be veal, are frequently sold in the market.

Have your butcher bone and roll the roast, and freeze the bones for future use in making stock.

Rub roast with garlic clove, then insert clove in a slit in the meat. Rub meat with salt, flour, pepper, rosemary, and lovage.

Pour olive oil into a flat casserole, and set roast in casserole. Lay thin slices of salt pork on top of roast. (Veal has very little fat.)

Set roast in oven on high heat for first ¼ hour, then reduce heat to 350°. Remove roast from oven until oven heat has gone down. Then add water and roast, 30–35 minutes to the pound, basting frequently, and adding more water if necessary.

About an hour before roast is done, add wine and capers and continue basting.

The gravy for the veal roast:

½ cup Rhine wine
2 tablespoons potato flour
1 teaspoon paprika
few grains cayenne pepper
drippings in casserole
1 teaspoon capers

Mix wine with flour, paprika, and cayenne pepper. Bring the drippings to a boil in a skillet, add flour mixture and capers, and stir rapidly until gravy thickens.

Serve with **Potatoes au Gratin, Zucchini Squash Sautéed No. 1, Cucumber Ginger Pickles, Red and Green Salad,** and, for dessert, **Mint Brandied Peaches.**

## HUNGARIAN VEAL GOULASH

2 cups cubed carrots
2 medium potatoes, peeled and cubed
3 medium onions, quartered
6 mushrooms, minced
1 pound veal, cut in 1-inch cubes
4 tablespoons flour
6 tablespoons butter
salt to taste
1 teaspoon black peppercorns
½ dozen coriander seeds
2 tablespoons paprika
2 bay leaves
2 teaspoons chopped marjoram or origanum leaves
½ teaspoon chopped thyme leaves
½ teaspoon chopped basil leaves

Parboil vegetables and mushrooms in salted water to cover, and reserve stock.

Place veal in bag with flour and shake well. Heat 4 tablespoons of butter in skillet, add meat, sprinkle with salt, and sauté until meat is brown; then add vegetable stock and stir in the flour remaining in the bag.

Grease a casserole with the remaining tablespoons of butter. Turn meat and vegetables and the juice into the casserole. Add peppercorns, coriander, paprika, bay leaves, and fresh herbs. Mix well. Cover casserole and simmer in 300° oven for approximately 2 hours.

Serves 8.

Serve with **Shallot Bread** and a green herb salad.

## LEFTOVER VEAL LUNCHEON

This makes a light luncheon dish.

2 tablespoons butter
2 tablespoons olive oil
1 medium-sized potato, peeled and "julienned"
salt and pepper
2 thin slices large Bermuda onion
4 slices leftover veal roast
5 rosemary leaves, chopped fine
¼ teaspoon powdered ginger

Heat butter and olive oil in skillet. Add potatoes, sprinkle with salt and pepper to taste, and brown, turning frequently. Spread potatoes on paper towels to remove excess grease.

Sauté onion until golden brown in same fat, in skillet. Remove onions, pour drippings from skillet into a casserole, and arrange the veal in the casserole with the onions on top of the meat and the potatoes on top of the onions. Sprinkle with rosemary and ginger and bake in oven preheated to 350° until heated through.

Serves 4.

Serve with a green herb salad and **Sherry Mushrooms.**

A succulent way to cook lamb is to braise it. In the days before modern cooking fuels, braising was done in a deep iron or copper casserole called a *braisière,* with a heavy lid, shaped to hold charcoal. The roast was set in the *braisière* with a small amount of liquid, and covered. Then the metal casserole was set on top of the coal or wood stove, or on live coals in a fireplace, coals were heaped on the lid, and heat came from above and below. The meat simmered and roasted simultaneously.

Today, what is commonly called a Dutch oven, a deep heavy iron skillet with a heavy lid, is used for braising. The cook must first brown the meat in the open pan on top of the stove, then add a small amount of liquid, water and/or wine, with the seasonings. The lid is put on and the Dutch oven set in the electric or gas oven to complete the braising.

## BRAISED STUFFED SHOULDER OF LAMB

1 lamb shoulder, approximately 9 pounds
2 slices bread
salt and pepper
1 egg
2 teaspoons fresh, chopped mint leaves
2 teaspoons chopped lemon-balm leaves
2 teaspoons curry
1 tablespoon honey
3 tablespoons port wine
flour
1 clove garlic
4 tablespoons butter

Have your butcher remove the bones from the lamb shoulder, and freeze the bones for future use. With the bones removed, the shoulder will weigh about half the amount of the unboned meat, 4½ pounds. Have the butcher roll and tie the meat.

Crumble bread. Add 1 teaspoon salt, 1 teaspoon pepper, the egg, herbs, curry, honey, and wine. Mix well. Partly unroll roast by cutting the strings, except on one end. Spread stuffing on inside of roll. Reroll and tie meat again with string, or skewer.

Rub roast with flour, salt, and pepper. Quarter a garlic clove and insert in four small slits in meat.

Heat butter in lower half of Dutch oven. Brown meat on all sides, add 1 cup water, and put lid on oven. Set Dutch oven in preheated, 300° oven. When water starts to simmer reduce heat to 250° and cook for 3 hours, or 40–45 minutes to the pound.

Serves 8.

Serve with **Mange-Tout Peas, Red Cabbage,** and, for dessert, **Rose Almond Soup.**

## LEFTOVER BRAISED LAMB

butter
2 medium onions, ringed
2 cups cooked lamb, cut in ¾-inch cubes
1 cup carrots, cut in small chunks
¾ cup rutabaga, peeled and cubed
1 medium-sized potato, peeled and diced
1 teaspoon salt
2 tablespoons curry
2 tablespoons potato flour or cornstarch
2 cups milk
½ cup Rhine wine
corn meal

Grease the casserole with 2 tablespoons butter. Arrange a layer of onion rings on the bottom, then a layer of meat, next carrots, turnips, meat again, and the remaining vegetables and meat, layer on layer. Top with the potatoes.

Mix salt, curry, and thickening with milk and wine and pour this over meat and vegetables. Sprinkle with corn meal. Bake in a covered casserole in an oven preheated to 350° for 40 minutes. Reduce heat to 225°. Bake 1 hour more. Remove cover, dot the lamb casserole with butter, turn oven up to 250°, and bake until top is brown.

Serves 6.

Serve with a **Red and Green Salad.**

## BRAISED LAMB SHANKS

2 lamb shanks
flour
salt and pepper
butter
½ teaspoon fresh, chopped rosemary leaves
1 teaspoon fresh, finely chopped mint leaves
2 cloves garlic
2 Italian frying peppers or 1 bell pepper
1 large baking potato, cut lengthwise in eighths
12 shallots or 6 small onions
1 wineglass sherry

Dredge the shanks on all sides with flour. Sprinkle with salt and pepper. Brown the meat in butter, in the bottom half of an iron Dutch oven. When brown, remove pan from stove, sprinkle on the herbs, and insert a clove of garlic in the meat of each shank, securing the cloves with toothpicks. Add about a cup of water to the skillet, cover, set in an oven preheated to 350°, and cook about 1 hour.

Cut off tops of peppers, remove seeds and pith, and slice in rings. Add peppers and other vegetables and cook about 1 hour more, or until meat is tender and vegetables done. Pour on sherry and let simmer about 5 minutes.

Serves 2.

Serve with a green herb salad with a **Sour-Cream Dressing.**

## LAMB STEW AND RAW-POTATO DUMPLINGS

**The Stew**

1 pound stewing lamb, bone in
1 cup shallots
salt
2 carrots, cut in 1-inch chunks
2 teaspoons minced dill
2 teaspoons capers
¼ cup Rhine wine
½ teaspoon black peppercorns
⅛ cup milk
1 tablespoon cornstarch

Have butcher cut meat in 1½-inch pieces.

Break shallots into cloves and peel. Place meat, shallots and 1 teaspoon salt in an enameled iron cocotte, with water, not quite to cover. Bring water to boil, put lid on cocotte, and let lamb simmer over low heat until meat is nearly done (about 1 hour).

Add carrots, dill, capers, wine, peppercorns, and salt to taste. Mix milk with cornstarch and stir in.

**The Raw-Potato Dumplings**

1 potato
½ cup flour
½ teaspoon baking soda
¼ teaspoon salt
⅛ teaspoon pepper
⅛ teaspoon minced rosemary leaves
2 teaspoons milk

Peel and mince the potato in the meat grinder, finest grind. Mix potato with flour, baking soda, salt and pepper, rosemary and milk. Mold into dumplings, about half the size of a golf ball. The dumplings should be the consistency of bread dough, and not too soft.

Place dumplings on *top* of meat and vegetables in the lamb stew. Do not mix them into the gravy. Cover kettle, and cook about ½ hour, or until dumplings are done.

Serves 6.

Serve with a green herb salad.

## SHOULDER LAMB CHOPS

salt and pepper
1 teaspoon minced dill
½ teaspoon minced rosemary leaves
3 shoulder lamb chops
flour
1 egg
corn meal
1 tablespoon butter
½ cup sauterne

Rub salt and pepper and the herbs into both sides of the lamb chops. Then rub lightly on each side with flour.

Beat egg with wire whisk. Dip chops in egg, coating them thoroughly; then sprinkle corn meal on both sides.

Melt butter in an iron skillet. Place chops in skillet and set in preheated, 375° oven. Bake until brown. Then pour on wine and cook about 15 minutes longer, basting frequently.

Serves 3.

Serve with **Baked Acorn Squash** and **Everyday Cucumber Pickles.**

## SAUTÉED LAMB KIDNEYS AUX CHANTERELLES

4 lamb kidneys
salt
1 teaspoon herb vinegar
1 8-ounce can chanterelle mushrooms
4 tablespoons butter
pepper
½ cup peeled, sliced shallots
flour
¼ cup Madeira wine
¼ teaspoon ginger
¼ teaspoon whole coriander seeds
1 teaspoon fresh, chopped basil leaves

Chanterelles, listed by authorities as one of the very best edible mushrooms, have funnel-shaped caps which are egg-yolk yellow in color. The flesh is white. They are, of course, better to use fresh than canned, and can be bought fresh in European markets, but we have not seen them for sale in America except in cans. Those imported from France are marked *"chanterelles"*; those from Germany, *"Pfifferlinge."*

In season, we pick them fresh from the woods, where they grow wild. If you are a good amateur mycologist, you will do likewise, but we wish to caution anyone who knows only the common field mushrooms against picking wild chanterelles. The saffron-yellow, poisonous jack-o'-lantern mushroom can be mistaken for a chanterelle by one who does not know mushrooms. And boiling with a silver spoon to see if the silver tarnishes is *not* a test of the edibility of a fungus.

To return to our recipe, slice kidneys in halves; cut out and discard hard, fatty core. Then slice the kidneys crosswise, in ¼-inch strips. Cover with water, add 1 teaspoon salt and the vinegar, and soak for ½ hour.

Drain juice from mushroom can, and set juice aside. Sauté mushrooms in 2 tablespoons butter for 5 minutes. Sprinkle with salt and pepper and place in a bowl. Sauté shallots until golden, and set in bowl with the mushrooms. Drain kidneys, discard water, and dry meat on paper towels. Sprinkle kidneys with flour and keep turning until well covered. Sauté for 5 minutes in the frying pan in which mushrooms and shallots were cooked, adding remaining butter. Pour on wine and mushroom juice, add the mushrooms and the shallots, the ginger, the coriander, and the basil, and simmer 10 minutes more.

Serves 3.

Serve on a platter around a mound of riced potatoes, with **Shallot Bread,** cucumber salad, and **Ginger Beans.**

## ROAST LOIN OF PORK

A savory, juicy recipe.

1 4-pound, 7-rib, pork loin
1 tablespoon butter
2 big cloves shallots, quartered
1 young tender rosemary sprig, 4 inches long
salt
pepper
1 teaspoon finely chopped lovage leaves
1 teaspoon finely chopped sage leaves
1 small onion
1 teaspoon powdered ginger
2 tablespoons pineapple juice
2 teaspoons brown sugar
1 cup sauterne
2 cups sliced apples
½ teaspoon cinnamon
2 tablespoons flour
2 tablespoons sherry

Wipe meat and score fat with a knife. Melt butter in roasting pan. Remove pan from fire and set roast in pan, fat side up. Make an incision, 4 inches long, 1 inch deep, in top of loin; insert the shallots and rosemary; and skewer. Rub fat side of roast with salt, pepper, lovage, and sage. Mince the onion, then crush it with a wooden spoon and spread it on the top of the roast. Sprinkle on the ginger, pineapple juice, and brown sugar, and pat it all down.

Pour sauterne and 1 cup water into the pan, not onto the roast. Preheat the oven to 500°, and roast the pork at this heat for ¼ hour. Remove roast, baste, and reduce heat in oven to 350° before returning meat. Roast at this heat for 2 hours,

20 minutes, basting frequently, and turning the meat four times, so that the bottom, the bone side, will be browned, as is the fat side, and the juices will have a chance to penetrate the loin.

Cook the apples in a saucepan with the cinnamon. Place roast on a serving casserole, surrounded with the apples. Blend flour with the sherry and the juices in the roasting pan, and pour this over the roast. Set roast in oven. When juice thickens, meat is ready to serve.

Serves 7.

Serve with **Crookneck Squash**, yams, and **Everyday Cucumber Pickles.**

## JAMBON AUX POIRES

1 precooked ham, butt end, about 6 pounds
cloves
½ cup brown sugar
1 teaspoon mustard flour (dry mustard)
1 teaspoon powdered ginger
2 teaspoons minced spearmint leaves
1 teaspoon minced pineapple-sage leaves
2 Bosc pears
1 cup sauterne
cinnamon

Dot ham with cloves. Place ham, fat side up, in roasting pan. Mix sugar, mustard, ginger, and herbs together in a cup. Quarter pears, remove seeds, stem, and flower end, and cut in thin slices, but do not peel.

Pour wine over ham, spread on sugar mixture, and cross-hatch with lines of cinnamon. Arrange pears around ham. Roast in a 350° oven, until sugar is brown and the pears soft (about 1½ hours). Then baste, place most of pear strips on top of ham, and roast 10 minutes more.

Serve with **Julienne Peppers, Sour-Cream Potato Salad,** and **A Dessert Fruit Salad.**

To use some of the leftover ham, make:

## EGGS A LA BENEDICT

4 English muffins, sliced in halves
8 circles of roast ham, same size as the English muffins
8 eggs
salt
Hollandaise sauce

To be at its best, eggs and Hollandaise sauce should be made ready simultaneously. A confederate to poach the eggs and toast the muffins, while you do the Hollandaise, makes this recipe quick and easy; but lacking help, proceed as follows.

Slice the muffins and the ham, then prepare ingredients for the Hollandaise.

## HERB HOLLANDAISE SAUCE

1 teaspoon finely chopped parsley
½ teaspoon finely chopped chervil
few grains cayenne pepper
⅛ teaspoon salt
1 egg yolk
1 bar (½ cup) butter, cut in thirds
1 teaspoon lemon juice
2 teaspoons tarragon vinegar

First chop and mix the herbs with the cayenne pepper and salt and set aside. Separate the egg.

Set a double boiler on the stove to heat. Select a saucepan at least 3½ inches deep for poaching the eggs. Part of the secret of making good poached eggs lies in the deep pan. Fill the pan about three quarters' full of lightly salted water, and bring to a boil on the stove, then reduce heat until water just simmers.

Eggs simmered do not separate. On the contrary, the whites jell close to, and all over, the yolk.

By now the water in the lower half of the double boiler should be hot. Put a third of the butter in the top of the boiler with the lemon juice and the egg yolk, and whip it, not too fast, with a wire whisk until the butter melts. Then add the second piece of butter, keep whisking, and when it melts, add the last piece of butter. Then stir until all butter is melted and sauce is reduced to the desired consistency. Mix in the tarragon vinegar, and remove from the stove, but leave over the hot water in the double boiler to keep warm. Toast the English muffins, then top each half muffin with a slice of ham and a poached egg and spoon on the Hollandaise sauce.

P.S. If the sauce is stubborn and refuses to thicken—in other words, curdles—add a tablespoon, or, if necessary, 2 tablespoons, of cream and it should smooth out and thicken at once.

Serves 8.

Serve with a green herb salad with **Russian Herb Dressing.**

## CHICKEN WITH SOUR-CREAM GRAVY

1 3–4-pound broiler
flour
chicken fat
2 tablespoons olive oil
1 teaspoon salt
½ teaspoon black ground pepper
2 teaspoons fresh chopped tarragon leaves
¼ teaspoon **Mixed-Herb Vinegar**
⅓ cup Madeira wine
¼ cup cloves of shallots
1 tablespoon cornstarch or potato flour
4 tablespoons sour cream

Have butcher split broiler into halves. In ½ cup water, boil giblets and neck for stock. Remove excess fat that usually lies in the body cavity. Dredge chicken with flour, combine chicken fat and olive oil, and heat on top of stove in deep skillet. Place chicken in skillet, skin side up. Sprinkle with salt, pepper, and tarragon. Add vinegar, wine, and shallots. Set pan in oven, about 7 inches below broiler, and broil, basting frequently. Turn each half every 10 minutes, and broil until chicken is tender.

When juice in pan begins to get low, add giblet stock.

Mix cornstarch and sour cream and stir into the drippings in the pan for gravy. Baste gravy onto chicken and broil 3 minutes more.

Serves 2 hungry people.

Serve with **Zucchini Squash Sautéed No. 2, Mange-Tout Peas,** and a green herb salad.

## CHICKEN IN COCOTTE

1 4-pound, 4-ounce can whole cooked chicken
butter
1 pound large mushrooms
2 medium bell or 4 frying peppers
2 cups shallot cloves
4 tablespoons flour
8 young carrots, cubed and parboiled
3 teaspoons minced tarragon leaves
4 teaspoons curry
salt and pepper
3 eggs
bread crumbs

Pour stock out of can and reserve. Bone chicken, cut in small pieces, and set aside. Melt 5 tablespoons butter in cocotte over low heat. Slice mushroom stems crosswise and reserve caps.

Cut off stems, remove seeds and pith from peppers, and ring.

Turn up heat under cocotte and sauté the mushroom stems, pepper, and shallots, until shallots are transparent. Remove cocotte from the stove. Stir flour into the chicken stock and add it, with the carrots and the tarragon.

Stir in curry and salt and pepper to taste. Mix all ingredients well, then add the chicken and stir lightly.

Whip eggs with a wire whisk and spread egg over top of other ingredients. Sprinkle with bread crumbs, arrange mushroom caps on top, and dot generously with butter.

Place cocotte under the broiler until mushroom caps are brown; then cover cocotte and place in a medium oven. Cook until ingredients jell.

Serves 10.

Serve with **Mange-Tout Peas**, buttered seashell macaroni, cooked according to directions on the package, and a green herb salad.

**CHICKEN GUMBO**

2 pounds chicken legs
flour
salt and pepper
olive oil
¼ cup peeled, chopped shallots
1½ cups okra, sliced in narrow rings
1 Italian green pepper, sliced lengthwise
⅓ cup chopped celery stalks
4 medium tomatoes, sliced
2 teaspoons chopped parsley leaves
1 teaspoon chopped tarragon leaves
½ teaspoon finely chopped lovage leaves
1 teaspoon paprika
1 cup cooked rice

Put chicken legs in a bag with flour, and shake until meat is dredged. Sprinkle with salt and pepper, and sauté the chicken in olive oil until brown. Remove chicken legs and arrange in a casserole greased with olive oil.

Place the shallots, okra, green pepper, celery, tomatoes, and herbs in skillet in which chicken was sautéed. Sprinkle with salt and pepper, and cook over slow heat about 15 minutes. Arrange these ingredients with chicken in casserole, add 1½ cups hot water, sprinkle on the paprika, and cook in 350° oven until chicken legs are tender. Add rice and serve.

Serves 8.

## CREAMED CHICKEN

4 medium-sized mushrooms
1 frying pepper
butter
salt and pepper
1 cup chicken stock
½ cup sour cream
2 teaspoons flour
2 teaspoons finely chopped parsley leaves
½ teaspoon finely chopped tarragon leaves
1 cup diced cooked chicken
1 teaspoon sherry
paprika

Slice mushroom stems crosswise, the caps vertically. Cut off stem end of pepper, remove pith and seeds, and slice in thin strips. Sauté pepper and mushrooms in butter and sprinkle with salt and pepper. When mushrooms are brown, mix stock with sour cream and flour. Put the stock, herbs, and the chicken, with the mushrooms and pepper, in the frying pan and let come to a boil. Stir until sauce thickens, then add sherry and sprinkle with paprika.

Serves 4.

Serve on toast, with Frenched snap beans.

## ROCK CORNISH GAME HENS AU SAUCE CHANTERELLE

12 Rock Cornish game hens, small size, eviscerated
24 large pitted prunes
12 fresh tarragon sprigs, each about 4 inches long
pepper
½ teaspoon salt
1 teaspoon chopped fresh rosemary leaves
flour
butter
2 4-ounce cans **chanterelle mushrooms**
1 cup chopped shallots
½ cup brandy

Into each little hen, place 2 prunes and 1 sprig of tarragon. (By a sprig, we mean a stem with leaves on it.)

Secure legs and wings of hens to body with string. Mix pepper and salt and rosemary with enough flour to dust the birds. Rub flour mixture over each one. Grease a roasting pan well with butter and set chickens, breast up, in pan. Dab each chicken breast with butter. Add the mushrooms and the shallots to the pan. Preheat oven to 450°. Place roasting pan in oven, and when chickens begin to brown, add 3 cups water, and lower heat. Baste frequently until done. Test by inserting a fork between the wing and the body of one of the chickens. If wing separates easily, they are done.

Pour brandy over chickens and cook about 2 minutes more.

Then make the chanterelle sauce as follows:

butter
1½ teaspoons sugar
2 tablespoons flour
½ cup milk
¼ cup cream
1 wineglass sherry
salt and pepper
12 ripe olives, cut in slices

Grease an iron skillet with butter and stir in sugar over high heat, until brown. Add flour and continue to stir rapidly until flour is brown. Blend milk and cream with flour and sugar. When sauce begins to thicken, add sherry and olives, and the shallots, mushrooms, and drippings from the roasting pan, salt and pepper to taste. Stir and cook until the right consistency.

Arrange chickens in a casserole and pour the chanterelle sauce over the chickens.

Serves 12.

Serve with **Savory Carrots,** Lima beans, a green herb salad, and **Mint Brandied Peaches** for dessert.

## TURKEY IN FOIL WITH MADEIRA GRAVY

First, the stuffing:

1 cup pitted prunes
1 cup peeled, cored, and diced apples
1 cup parboiled, diced potatoes
1 cup peeled shallots
4 mushrooms
4 slices bread
1 teaspoon minced sage leaves
2 teaspoons minced tarragon leaves

1 teaspoon minced thyme leaves
1 teaspoon salt
½ teaspoon pepper
1 egg
¼ cup milk

Put the prunes, apples, potatoes, shallots, mushrooms, and bread through the meat grinder. Mix well with the herbs, salt and pepper, the egg and the milk.

Now, the turkey:

1 Beltsville turkey
olive oil
⅛ pound butter
1 teaspoon finely chopped tarragon leaves
salt and pepper
flour
1 wineglass Madeira

Beltsville turkeys, the small breed developed at the Agricultural Experiment Station at Beltsville, Maryland, average 7–9 pounds in weight.

Stuff the turkey only about three quarters' full, because the apples and prunes swell during cooking. Sew or skewer, to hold stuffing in. Secure neck skin and tie down wings.

Cover wing tips and end of leg bones with small pieces of foil, to prevent sharp bones from piercing main foil. Cut piece of heavy cooking foil, large enough to allow overlap of 3 inches on the turkey's breast. Coat foil lightly with olive oil. Set turkey on its back, on the greased side of the foil. Melt butter, add tarragon, and brush it all over the bird. Sprinkle with salt, pepper and flour. Fold the foil tightly around the bird, place breast up in roasting pan, and cook about 2½ hours, starting at 450° preheated oven. During the last 20 minutes, fold back the foil. Pour wine over turkey, reduce heat to 350°, and let brown, basting frequently.

To make the Madeira Gravy:

giblets and neck
1 teaspoon ginger
1 teaspoon fresh minced savory leaves
1 teaspoon Hungarian paprika
3 teaspoons cornstarch
½ cup light cream
2 teaspoons butter
¼ teaspoon sugar
salt and pepper
¼ cup Maderia wine

Boil giblets and neck for stock. Cut meat off neck, mince the giblets and the neck meat. Stir ginger, savory, and paprika into stock. Blend cornstarch into cream and add to stock.

Melt butter in skillet, brown the sugar, stirring rapidly, and add the minced giblets and meat, the stock, and salt and pepper to taste. Simmer, stirring constantly, until gravy thickens. Then pour in wine, and simmer a minute more.

Serves 8.

Serve with **Rutabaga,** creamed shallots, **Acorn Squash,** a green herb salad, and **Angel Frappé,** for dessert.

For a treat, substitute **lingonberries** for the cranberries traditionally served with turkey in the United States.

## LINGONBERRIES

The large bog cranberries (*Vaccinium macrocarpon*), the common cranberry, are native only to America. They grow wild in bogs in cooler sections of the United States and Canada, and are raised extensively on a commercial basis. These are the cranberries that caused such a furor a few days before

Thanksgiving, 1959, when the secretary of the Department of Health, Education, and Welfare announced that some crops had been contaminated by the weed killer with the tongue-twisting name "Amino Triazole."

Lingonberries (*Vaccinium vitis-idaea*) are low-bush, small, mountain cranberries that grow wild in rocky soil in northern America, Europe, and Asia. They are a little more delicate in flavor and slightly more tart than the bog cranberries.

Most of the lingonberries sold in the American market come from Newfoundland. Both canned and fresh are carried by Scandinavian food shops in America.

Now, the lingonberry sauce.

4 cups fresh lingonberries
2 cups sugar
1 cinnamon stick about 2½ inches long
pinch of salt

Let 2 cups water come to a boil. Add berries, sugar, cinnamon, and salt. Cook for 20 minutes, stirring constantly, to prevent sticking. Skim off foam as it forms. Pack in jars and keep refrigerated.

Makes about 3½ cups.

## SMOKED TURKEY

1 medium-sized smoked turkey
butter
2 tablespoons molasses
4 teaspoons fresh, chopped tarragon leaves
cinnamon
4 teaspoons powdered ginger
6 bananas
2 cups white wine

Most smoked turkeys are tough and very salty. Therefore, parboil the bird for about 2 hours and discard the water. Then place the turkey, breast side up, in a come-to-the-table, buttered casserole. Smear molasses on breast and legs and sprinkle with the tarragon, cinnamon, and ginger. Peel and slice the bananas crosswise, and arrange in pan around the turkey.

Add wine and ½ cup of water. Set roasting pan in oven, at 350° preheat, and roast until turkey is brown. Baste frequently. Time for roasting: about 20 minutes.

Serve with **Broiled Mushroom Caps, Chard Greens,** and **Okra aux Échalotes.**

## HOLIDAY GOOSE

First, the goose stuffing.

- 2 cups shelled chestnuts
- 1 pound mushrooms
- ¼ cup peeled, minced shallots
- 2 frying peppers
- 4 slices bread
- 1 cup sour cream
- 1 egg
- 3 tablespoons finely chopped parsley
- 1 teaspoon finely chopped thyme leaves
- 1 teaspoon salt
- ½ teaspoon pepper

After preparing chestnuts, by boiling in water to cover over a low fire until soft, then removing shells and skin, put the nuts through a meat grinder, finest grind.

Slice mushroom stems crosswise; the caps, vertically. Add shallots. Cut off stem end of peppers, remove pith and seeds, and mince. Crumble bread into the sour cream, and add the egg. Combine with the other ingredients and knead well.

Now, the holiday goose:

1 8–9-pound domestic goose
flour
salt and pepper
1 teaspoon finely chopped origanum leaves
olive oil
6 apples
brown sugar
1 teaspoon ginger
1 cup white wine

Line the roasting pan with a generous piece of cooking foil, enough to fold over 3 inches on breast of goose. Remove loose fat from goose and set aside. Stuff and truss goose. Rub with flour, salt and pepper, and origanum.

Brush a little olive oil on the foil where the goose will rest, to prevent sticking. Set goose on foil, breast up. Cut fat in thin strips and lay on the breast. Fold the foil over the bird tightly.

Place roasting pan in hot oven preheated to 450°, and roast for about 2½ hours. Fold back foil and set goose in a come-to-the-table casserole.

Drain the juices from the foil into the roasting pan itself. Now skim the fat that will be floating on top of the juice and reserve it, for goose fat is excellent to use for sautéing. Put about 2 cups of the stock in the casserole with the goose.

Core the apples and set three on each side of the goose. Sprinkle the apples with brown sugar and ginger. Add wine to casserole, and roast in a moderate oven until apples are baked and the goose tender and brown. Baste frequently. Just before removing from the oven, sprinkle a little brown sugar on the goose, and when sugar caramelizes, serve.

Serve with **Kohlrabi en Casserole, Savory Carrots, Cucumber Ginger Pickles, Lingonberries,** and **Champagne Compote** for dessert.

# 8. FROM THE FISH MARKET

Unlike the fisherman with a rod, who must wait for a strike, the fisherman who goes to the market has spread before him a delightful variety of sea food, everything from green (uncooked) shrimp, to fillet of sole. The first question is, should you buy fresh or frozen?

The answer to this is quite different from that given for meat. Step up to the unfrozen-sea-food department. There is nothing comparable to a fresh fish platter, especially when complemented by fresh herbs. However, look the fresh fish squarely in the eye, and if the eye is sunken and "gone," you will be better off buying frozen fish. Fresh fish must be almost flopping on the counter to have that exquisite, sea-song, salty tang, and to retain the texture associated with the fresh product. Not that fish that have been preserved on ice for quite a long time are bad, but they have lost their superiority to the frozen product. Motto: Buy very, very fresh, or frozen.

Frozen fish have one great advantage over the fresh. They do not have to be cooked at once, and, like frozen meats, you can store them in your freezer, and because of this, you can get good buys on bargain days and look forward to a wealth of good sea-food meals during Lent, and when the dill and fennel are ready in the garden.

One kind of shellfish we nearly always buy frozen, however, is shrimp. If green shrimp are kept for long, merely iced, they begin to smell so strong that not even the combined efforts of dill and tarragon vinegar can staunch the kitchen odors. And in our opinion, frozen shrimp are equal in flavor to the fresh. Note also that uncooked frozen shrimp, with shells on, will shrink almost to half of their weight when thawed, shelled, and cooked. So if you want to serve a pound, buy two pounds.

A word on how much fish to order for a meal. In general, for steak-and-roast-beef Americans, plan on a quarter of a pound of fish per person. If, however, your guests are Scandinavian, serve a half pound per person.

So much for general shop talk. If you wish to experiment with herbs for your own favorite fish recipes, consult the **Flavor Chart** for the herbs which have a special affinity for fish and shellfish.

We lead off our recipes for fish with a fish that was formerly sold in few markets, namely fresh-water trout. In recent years trout have become not only plentiful but cheap. These trout are not caught in the open stream or lake but raised on trout farms and quick-frozen for the mass market. This has brought a delectable fresh-water game fish into Everyman's kitchen.

## TROUT AU BEURRE NOIR

2 frozen rainbow trout, about 10 ounces
1 teaspoon fresh, chopped tarragon leaves
½ teaspoon finely chopped lemon-balm leaves
¼ teaspoon finely chopped rosemary leaves
1 teaspoon herb vinegar
2 tablespoons butter
salt and pepper
1 teaspoon lemon juice

Let trout thaw at room temperature. Mix the herbs with the vinegar, and put half in each trout. Heat 1 tablespoon butter in heavy iron skillet, sprinkle trout lightly with salt and pepper, and sauté, turning frequently, to brown both sides. Remove fish from skillet. Heat second tablespoon butter in the pan, stirring constantly, until butter is brown. Do not let burn. Add the lemon juice and pour over trout.

Serves 2.

Serve with **Basil Potatoes, Mange-Tout Peas,** and an **Avocado Salad.**

## FILLET OF SOLE À L'ESTRAGON

2 tablespoons butter
1 pound fillet of sole
paprika
salt and pepper
1 hard-boiled egg, chopped fine
2 teaspoons finely chopped estragon (tarragon) leaves
2 tablespoons flour
¼ cup light cream
1 bay leaf
⅔ cup Rhine wine
1 teaspoon basil vinegar

Grease skillet with 1 tablespoon butter. Brown fillet on one side on top of the stove. Sprinkle with paprika, salt, and pepper. Dot with the remaining butter and set under broiler until brown. Remove fillet to lightly greased casserole and place in warming oven.

Mix the egg with the tarragon and set aside. Blend flour with the cream and ½ cup water and put in pan in which fish was cooked. Add bay leaf, and salt and pepper to taste. Set over medium heat on top of stove and stir until sauce thickens. Be sure not to let it burn. Add wine and vinegar, cook over fire about 2 minutes; then add the egg and cook 1 minute longer, stirring constantly. Remove bay leaf and pour sauce over fish in the casserole.

Serves 4.

Serve with **Savory Carrots, Potatoes au Gratin,** and a tomato salad.

## BROILED COD

1 pound fillet of cod
½ teaspoon finely chopped savory leaves
½ teaspoon finely chopped tarragon leaves
3 tablespoons corn meal
3 tablespoons butter
salt and pepper
¼ cup Rhine wine

Many of the cod fillets are not too well boned, and so make certain that all bones are removed before cooking.

Mix the herbs with the corn meal, and rub on both sides of the fillet. Heat half the butter in an iron skillet, place cod in pan, and dot top of fish with remaining butter. Sauté 1 minute on top of stove. Then broil cod until brown. Pour wine over fish, broil a few minutes more, basting frequently.

Serves 4.

Serve with snap beans, parsley potatoes (make the same as **Basil Potatoes,** substituting parsley for the basil), and **Fresh Herb Salad No. 2.**

## SHAD

1 fillet of shad
butter
4 sprigs fresh fennel leaves
1 sprig fresh tarragon
3 sprigs fresh thyme
salt and pepper
flour
1 egg
¼ cup milk
bread crumbs
paprika
¼ cup white wine

Shad is a strong fish of the herring family and sweet herbs reduce the fishiness, both in the odor of the cooking and in the taste.

Rub the fillet on both sides with butter and lay it skin side down on a plate. Place the sprigs of fennel in the fold where the main bone has been removed in the process of filleting. Strip leaves off stems of tarragon and thyme and scatter over the shad. Sprinkle with salt and pepper to taste and dust with flour. Transfer to well-buttered, preheated iron skillet.

Mix egg with milk and pour it on the fish, scooping it constantly from the sides of the pan onto the fish, to seal in the fresh herbs. When egg jells, sprinkle with bread crumbs and shut off heat, but leave pan on stove. Dot with butter and sprinkle with paprika.

Set iron skillet in oven about 8 inches below the broiler. When fish starts to get brown, reduce heat, pour on wine, and leave in oven until wine is reduced to about half, approximately 15 minutes.

Serves 4.

Serve with **Cauliflower Casserole,** mashed potatoes, and a **Red and Green Salad.**

## BROILED HADDOCK AUX FINES HERBES

1 pound fillet of haddock
¼ pound butter
mashed potatoes (made from 3 medium-sized potatoes)
2 teaspoons finely chopped fennel leaves
½ teaspoon finely chopped tarragon leaves
¼ teaspoon finely chopped rosemary leaves
1 egg
1 tablespoon flour
1 tablespoon paprika
salt and pepper
1 tablespoon sherry
2 tablespoons white wine

See that all bones are removed from the fillet. Poach fish in shallow pan in salted water, not quite to cover, for 4 minutes. Remove fish and place skin side down in well-buttered casserole. Surround with the mashed potatoes. Mix the herbs with the egg and spread on the fish. Sprinkle on the flour and dot with butter. Place casserole in oven, about 6 inches under broiler. When brown, sprinkle with paprika and salt and pepper and cook 1 more minute. Then pour on wine and broil 2 minutes. Remove from oven and cover with aluminum foil. Keep in warm oven until ready to serve.

Serves 4.

Serve with **Zucchini Squash Sautéed No. 2,** and **Fresh Herb Salad No. 1.**

## BROILED SCROD

1 egg
1 teaspoon salt
pepper
¼ cup flour
1 fillet of scrod (young cod or haddock)
bread crumbs
⅛ pound butter
½ teaspoon finely chopped dill leaves
½ teaspoon finely chopped thyme leaves
½ cup sherry
1 teaspoon lemon juice

Beat egg, salt, and pepper together in a bowl. Put flour in paper bag and drop fish into it. Shake well to coat fish with flour. Remove scrod and dip it in the egg. Put bread crumbs in another bag and roll the fish in the crumbs.

Melt butter in frying pan and lay fish in it, skin side down. If any egg mixture is left, pour over fish. Sprinkle with the herbs. Sauté for about 3 minutes over a hot fire. Place pan under the broiler. Baste frequently. When starting to brown, pour on the wine and keep on basting until fish is well browned.

Transfer the fish and the juice to a come-to-the-table casserole. Sprinkle on lemon juice, cover with foil, and place in warming oven until ready to serve.

Serves 4.

Serve with **Creamed Fennel au Vin Blanc,** Lima beans, and an upland-cress salad with **French Herb Dressing.**

## HADDOCK EN CASSEROLE AU VIN BLANC

4 medium-sized potatoes, peeled and boiled
¼ cup light cream
¼ pound butter
2 teaspoons chopped fennel leaves
salt and pepper
1 pound fillet of haddock
1 teaspoon finely chopped tarragon leaves
¼ teaspoon finely chopped rosemary leaves
1 egg
1 tablespoon flour
paprika
2 tablespoons sauterne
1 tablespoon sherry
1 lemon, cut in wedges

Mash the potatoes with the cream, 2 tablespoons butter, and the chopped fennel, and season with salt and pepper.

Make certain all bones have been removed from the fillet. Cut fish lengthwise in 6-inch lengths, and poach in water, just enough to cover fish, for 4 minutes. Remove fish from water and place skin side down in the center of a well-buttered, flat casserole. Arrange mashed potatoes around the fish and scallop with a spoon. Beat the tarragon and the rosemary into the egg and spread on the fish. Sprinkle with flour, dot with the remaining butter, and place in the oven about 6 inches below the broiler. When slightly brown, sprinkle with paprika and broil 1 minute more. Pour on the wine. Keep under the broiler about 2 more minutes, and then arrange lemon wedges on top of fish.

If you do not wish to serve the dish immediately, cover with foil and keep in warm oven.

Serves 4.

Serve with **Crookneck Squash, Kohlrabi en Casserole,** and a cucumber, chive, and lettuce salad.

## BAKED SWORDFISH STEAK

A handsome dish.

5 slices lean bacon
1 swordfish steak, boned, 3 inches thick (about 5 pounds)
flour
2 teaspoons finely chopped fennel leaves
salt and pepper
1 cup Rhine wine
6 shallots
½ pound mushrooms, chopped very fine
1 teaspoon finely chopped savory leaves
1 teaspoon paprika
1 hard-boiled egg

Line an oblong casserole with heavy aluminum foil. Cut bacon strips in halves and lay five pieces in a row on the foil. Rub steak all over with flour and set it on bacon in the casserole. Sprinkle the top of the fish with fennel, a little salt (bacon will supply some salt), and pepper. Lay the five remaining pieces of bacon on top of the steak and pour wine and ½ cup water into the casserole. Peel outer brown skin off shallots and break into cloves. Add shallots, mushrooms, and savory to wine.

Bake in an oven preheated to 350°. For an unfrozen steak, allow about 25–30 minutes to the pound. If the pan dries out, add more water.

When done, sprinkle the paprika in pencil-thin bands over the steak. Set under broiler for a few minutes to brown the top of the fish; then chop the egg and decorate the steak.

Serves 12.

Serve with **Baked Butternut Squash, Basil Potatoes, Everyday Cucumber Pickles,** and for dessert, **Pears Flambée.**

## SALMON IN COURT BOUILLON

1 2-pound salmon steak
1 teaspoon white-wine vinegar (tarragon)
1 *bouquet garni:* 2 sprigs tarragon, 2 sprigs parsley, 1 sprig thyme, 2 sprigs dill
1 bay leaf
12 coriander seeds
24 peppercorns
1 whole fennel
8 shallots, peeled
2 carrots, sliced thinly crosswise
salt and pepper
½ cup Rhine wine
4 grape leaves
½ teaspoon lemon juice

Court bouillon is an old French method, using herbs (as we do vinegar and dill when boiling shrimp) to allay the fishy odors of cooking fish, and at the same time to add a piquant flavor to the fish itself. Some standard recipes call for discarding the carrots and shallots after the fish is cooked, but why not garnish them around the salmon?

Now for the recipe. Rinse the salmon, and place it in a piece of cheesecloth, loosely tied at the top to make a bag. Set in a pot and cover salmon with water. Add vinegar. Tie the fresh herbs, the bay leaf, coriander, and peppercorns in a small cheesecloth bag and place in the pot. Strip off and discard the outer stringy leaves of the fennel, slice fennel crosswise, and add. Add vegetables and salt and pepper to pot, bring water to a boil, and let simmer 20 minutes. Add wine, grape leaves, and lemon juice, and simmer 5 more minutes. Dip out ½ cup of stock and let cool.

Take salmon out of cheesecloth, remove grape leaves, and

place them on bottom of a buttered casserole. Set salmon on grape leaves. Split salmon, remove the bone, and keep fish in warm oven.

Simmer stock until vegetables are done. Then arrange vegetables around the salmon in the casserole. Continue to simmer stock until about a pint remains. Meanwhile make the sauce.

2 teaspoons flour
½ cup cold stock
2 hard-boiled eggs
1 cup hot stock
1 cup minced parsley
1 tablespoon butter

(Refrigerate the remaining court bouillon for future use.)

Stir flour into ½ cup cold stock. Mash eggs with a fork and add to cold stock. Pour the cold and the hot stock into saucepan with the parsley; place over medium heat, and stir until sauce thickens. Add butter, and when butter melts, blend it in and pour sauce over fish.

Serves 6.

Serve with a salad featuring Chinese cabbage and peppers.

**BROILED ROCK LOBSTER**

2 frozen rock-lobster tails
3 tablespoons butter
⅛ teaspoon tarragon vinegar
2 sprigs fennel about as long as the lobster tails
salt and pepper
½ teaspoon brandy

Let lobster tails thaw at room temperature.

With a pair of kitchen shears, cut off and discard belly shells on lobster tails. Loosen meat from shell, all in one piece. It comes out very easily. (If the lobster is broiled while the meat is still attached to the shell, it is difficult to get the meat out.)

Melt 2 tablespoons butter, brush 1 tablespoon on inside of empty shells, then put back meat. Split meat down the center, but not all the way through. Sprinkle on the remaining melted butter and the vinegar and lay a sprig of fennel in each slit. Season with salt and pepper. Lay tails on their backs in skillet, shells down, and cook over low fire on top of stove for about 5 minutes. The butter which will spill out of the shells gives sufficient grease to prevent the tails from sticking. Remove pan from top of stove, put ¼ teaspoon brandy in slit in each tail, dot with the remaining butter (1 tablespoon), and broil.

Serves 2.

Serve with **Sautéed Artichoke Hearts, Mange-tout Peas,** and **Potatoes Baked.**

## CURRIED ROCK LOBSTER

15 frozen rock-lobster tails
6 sprigs dill, each about 6 inches long
2 teaspoons salt
½ pound butter
2 teaspoons curry
15 teaspoons sherry

Place frozen rock lobster in a saucepan with water to cover. Add dill and salt, and let water come to a boil. Boil 10 minutes. Dip lobster out of water and cool. Remove meat from the shells, and cut meat down center, as in previous recipe. Discard shells.

Melt 12 tablespoons (1½ bars) butter in a saucepan with curry, and set aside. Grease a skillet, add lobster, and dab on the remaining butter. Broil until meat is slightly brown.

Place 1 rock-lobster tail on each dinner plate; spoon 1 teaspoon sherry on each lobster tail, pour on hot curry butter, and serve immediately.

Serves 15.

Serve with **Potatoes au Gratin, Mange-tout Peas,** and an escarole salad with **Russian Herb Dressing.**

## SCALLOPS

1 pound scallops
salt
1 egg
2 teaspoons finely chopped tarragon leaves
2 tablespoons flour
2 tablespoons corn meal
pepper
⅛ pound butter
½ cup white wine

Simmer scallops in salted water, just enough to cover, for 5 minutes. Drain and set aside stock. Beat egg in a bowl with the tarragon. Put scallops in a paper bag with the flour, and shake until scallops are well coated. Drop scallops into the bowl with the egg, and turn with a fork until scallops are well covered with the egg. Then coat scallops with the corn meal.

Sprinkle with salt and pepper, and sauté scallops in butter, turning frequently so that they brown on all sides. When brown, add ½ cup scallop stock and wine, shaking the pan so that scallops get covered with the liquid.

Serves 4.

Serve with snap beans, **Zucchini Squash Sautéed No. 1,** and a cucumber salad with **Sour-Cream Dressing.**

*The length of time needed for the preparation of the following four shrimp recipes varies from quick to time consuming.*

**SHRIMPS NO. 1, IN SAUCE**

This is a quickie.

1½ pounds frozen green shrimp
1 teaspoon finely chopped dill leaves
1 teaspoon salt
1 teaspoon tarragon vinegar
3 shallots, peeled and chopped fine
2 tablespoons butter
1 tablespoon cornstarch or potato flour
2 tablespoons light cream
1 tablespoon sherry
⅛ teaspoon pepper

Boil frozen shrimp in water to cover, with dill, salt, and vinegar, until done, about 10 minutes. Strain off stock and reserve. Shell and devein shrimp.

Sauté shallots in 1 tablespoon butter until golden. Melt second tablespoon butter in a casserole and add shrimp. Blend cornstarch or potato flour with cream and ¾ cup cool shrimp stock. Add sherry and pepper. Pour sauce over shrimp, and place casserole over low heat on top of stove, turning shrimp now and then. Cook until sauce thickens.

Serves 4.

Serve with Lima beans, **Fennel Potatoes en Casserole,** and Imperial lettuce Waldorf salad with **Russian Herb Dressing.**

## SHRIMPS NO. 2, SURINAM SHRIMP

This is quite simple.

3 pounds Surinam shrimp
2 teaspoons tarragon vinegar
*bouquet garni:* 12 sprigs dill, 1 tarragon, each sprig about 8 inches long
salt and pepper
1 4-ounce can water chestnuts
2 cups snap beans, cut in ½-inch lengths
1 4-ounce can **chanterelle mushrooms**
1 tablespoon flour
¾ cup milk
4 hard-boiled eggs, chopped fine

Surinam is the trade name of tiny shrimp imported from South Africa. Each one is only about 1½ inches long, measured without the head. They are a great delicacy, but because they are so small, few cooks care to take the time to shell them. They are now offered on the market, shelled, deveined, and quick-frozen, and so are easy to prepare.

Place frozen shrimp in a pot not quite covered with water, and boil with vinegar, *bouquet garni,* and salt and pepper to taste, for 5 minutes after shrimp are thawed. Arrange shrimp on a platter.

Slice water chestnuts and add them with the snap beans and mushrooms to the stock. Boil until the beans are done. Blend flour into milk, cook in saucepan until thickened, and add the chopped eggs. Arrange water chestnuts, snap beans, and mushrooms on platter around the shrimp and pour on sauce.

Serves 8.

Serve with a green herb salad with **Sour-Cream Dressing.**

**SHRIMPS NO. 3, MARCO POLO**

This takes time to prepare.

5 pounds shrimp
*bouquet garni:* 12 sprigs dill, 2 tarragon, each sprig about 8 inches long
3 teaspoons tarragon vinegar
6 cups cut-up red tomatoes
3 teaspoons finely chopped marjoram or origanum leaves
3 teaspoons chopped basil leaves
¼ cup chopped celery stalks
6 teaspoons chopped parsley
⅓ cup chopped shallots
2 teaspoons salt
½ teaspoon freshly ground black pepper
1 tablespoon soya sauce
2 cups mushroom caps
1 tablespoon sugar
butter
2 tablespoons flour
2 teaspoons chili powder
1 box egg noodles
4 ounces grated Parmesan cheese

Boil shrimp in lightly salted water, with *bouquet garni* and the tarragon vinegar, not over 10 minutes. Shell and devein shrimp. Discard water. Slit each shrimp in two, lengthwise.

Mix tomatoes, origanum, basil, celery, parsley, shallots, salt and pepper, and soya sauce; let come to a boil, and boil for about 25 minutes, stirring occasionally. Then mash through a colander. Keep sauce in warm oven.

Cut up mushrooms crosswise in thin slices. Add sugar. Sauté

mushrooms in butter until brown. Add flour and chili powder to mushrooms, and stir; then add tomato sauce, and when sauce thickens, put in warm oven.

Now cook noodles according to directions on package, and arrange noodles in center of large serving platter. Place shrimp around noodles, and pour sauce over noodles and shrimp. Sprinkle Parmesan cheese over noodles only.

Serves 16.

Serve with chickory and roquette salad with **French Herb Salad Dressing.**

## SHRIMPS NO. 4, SHRIMP ORIENTALE

A one-dish supper, which takes time to prepare.

2 pounds shrimp
*bouquet garni,* sprigs about 4 inches long: 9 dill, 2 tarragon, 2 thyme
1 teaspoon tarragon vinegar
4 stalks celery
1 8-ounce can whole bamboo shoots
3 Italian sweet peppers or 2 bell peppers
½ pound mushroom buttons
1 5-ounce can hearts of palm
bread crumbs
butter
1 cup peeled shallots
1 1-pound can bean sprouts
potato flour or cornstarch

Place shrimp in rapidly boiling water, with *bouquet garni* and tarragon vinegar, and boil until done, about 10 minutes. Remove shrimp and set stock aside. Shell and devein shrimp and cut each in three pieces, crosswise. String celery and cut in narrow strips, about 4 inches long. Boil celery 10 minutes in 2 cups shrimp stock. This recipe, like most Oriental recipes, stresses texture, and celery should be undercooked rather than overcooked.

When celery is done, arrange it around the outer edge of a large, greased casserole.

Slice bamboo shoots (canned in quantities in Japan) and boil 5 minutes in stock in which celery was cooked. Add more stock if necessary. We boil the ingredients separately, one by one, so that each can be arranged separately on the platter, to make the dish look attractive.

Place bamboo shoots on the inner edge of the celery.

Then remove stem end and seeds and pith from peppers, slice in thin rings, and add, with the whole mushroom buttons, to the same boiling stock. Boil 5 minutes. Arrange peppers and mushrooms on the inner edge of the bamboo sprouts.

Hearts of palm, the tender shoots of palmettos, have a nut-like flavor. They are canned in Florida. Cut hearts of palms in about ¾-inch pieces, dust them with bread crumbs, and sauté in a buttered skillet until golden brown. Then arrange them on the inner edge of the mushrooms and peppers.

Slice shallots crosswise, and boil 10 minutes in stock, adding more stock as needed. Arrange shallots in the next ring, toward the center.

Drain bean sprouts, rinse in cold water to freshen, and bring to a boil in the hot stock. Stir 2 tablespoons potato flour or cornstarch into ⅔ cup cold shrimp stock, add cold stock to hot stock, and leave bean sprouts in. Boil until sauce thickens. Dip out bean sprouts and arrange in the center of the casserole. Reserve the thickened stock for the sauce. Make a mound of the shrimp on top of the bean sprouts.

The sauce:

1 tablespoon butter
1 teaspoon powdered ginger
1 teaspoon curry
2 teaspoons soya sauce
thickened stock

Heat butter in skillet in which hearts of palm were sautéed. Stir in lightly the ginger and the curry, add soya sauce, and the thickened stock, and let come to a boil. Pour sauce over the ingredients in the casserole.

Cover casserole with aluminum cooking foil, to prevent drying, and place in oven until warmed through.

Serves 8.

Serve with rice and an **Avocado Salad.**

## BROILED SHAD ROE

1 pair shad roe
salt and pepper
1 teaspoon finely chopped dill leaves
1 teaspoon finely chopped fennel leaves
½ teaspoon tarragon vinegar
bread crumbs
2 tablespoons butter
paprika
¼ cup white wine

Wash shad roe and remove white center membrane, but be careful not to tear the roe. Dry on paper towels. Poach roe in water to cover, on top of stove, with salt and pepper to taste, herbs, and vinegar, for about 5 minutes. Remove and roll roe in bread crumbs.

Melt 1 tablespoon butter in skillet and brown roe on one side on top of stove. Dab on remaining butter, sprinkle with paprika, and add wine and ¼ cup of water to skillet. Then set roe under the broiler until the upper side is brown, basting now and then. Do not broil too long or roe will dry out.

Serves 2.

Serve with **Scalloped Potatoes** and a tomato salad with **French Herb Salad Dressing.**

## SHAD-ROE OMELET

1 pair shad roe
6 sprigs dill, each about 12 inches long
6 eggs
6 tablespoons milk
1 teaspoon finely chopped chervil leaves
3 teaspoons finely chopped parsley leaves
4 teaspoons finely chopped fennel leaves
salt and pepper
butter

Poach roe with dill, in slightly salted water, for about 10 minutes. Discard dill. Remove roe, pull off loose membrane, and slice roe lengthwise in eight slices.

Break eggs into a bowl with the milk, chopped herbs, and salt and pepper, and beat with a fork. Grease frying pan well with butter. Heat pan, pour in egg mixture, and cook on top of stove until eggs begin to bubble. Remove pan from stove and arrange the roe on the half of the omelet away from the handle of the pan. Place pan under broiler. Do not let omelet brown. The minute the eggs get firm, remove pan from oven, tip pan away from you, and fold the half of the omelet nearest the handle of the pan over the roe. Serve immediately.

Serves 4.

Serve with **Mange-tout Peas.**

## ESCARGOTS (*SNAILS*)

Snails are customarily included in cookbooks under shellfish, because there are several kinds of edible sea snails, notably the periwinkle, the little snail often sold in England and France on pushcarts. The big sea whelk which looks like a conch is used mostly in soups.

The snails most commonly served in America, however, are land snails native to France, the Burgundy, or sometimes the small *petit gris*. They are now also raised in Louisiana in our country.

## ESCARGOT LUNCHEON

This makes a delicate, delightful, and satisfying meal.

- 2 dozen live snails, or 1 can precooked snails, shells included
- salt
- ¼ pound butter
- ½ clove garlic, minced
- 1 clove shallot, minced
- 2 teaspoons finely chopped parsley leaves
- pepper
- ½ teaspoon paprika

Gourmets prefer to buy live, rather than canned, precooked snails. The latter are easier to prepare, but when you have the time, and can buy fresh snails in the market, do so.

Live snails are sent to the market in a dormant state, the openings to their shells sealed with a thin, horny "door." But they are usually awake and walking all over the market basket by the time you buy them.

In any case, place them in heavily salted water, and let boil for not less than 20 minutes. Then remove snails from water, let cool, and fork them out of their shells. Cleanse shells well and scrub them with a wire brush.

The canned snail shells come in a separate container from the precooked snails and they are well scrubbed. Just open the can, drain off the liquid, and discard it. From there on, preparation of canned and fresh snails is the same.

Melt the butter, add the minced garlic and shallot and the chopped parsley. Sprinkle with pepper and salt.

Stuff each snail, tail first, back into its shell. Set shells on plates with openings up, a difficult feat on an ordinary plate. Special snail plates have small indentations the size of the bottom of a snail shell, and these hold shells upright. Fill each shell with the herb butter and sprinkle with paprika.

Spread the remaining herb butter on sesame-seed wafers (carried by most groceries). Heat snails and wafers in the oven together. Eat with snail picks.

Serves 3.

Serve hot with **Broiled Mushroom Caps, Sautéed Artichoke Hearts,** and an **Avocado Salad.**

# 9. THE BEGINNING AND END OF A MEAL

To spice up the cocktail hour, gather some herbs. We are not referring to the mint you use in juleps, or to the mint, borage, lemon balm, and pineapple sage which add a fragrant touch to iced summer teas and other drinks, but to the herbs with which a good cook can pep up canapés, those necessary garnishes to bourbon, scotch, and gin.

The herbs used in the canapé recipes, and the soup and dessert recipes which come after them, are to be found in both the Vegetable and Herb Garden and the Garden Salad Bowl and its Annex. The vegetables used in making the canapés are in the Vegetable and Herb Garden or the Garden Salad Bowl.

*Try fresh vegetables and sour cream.*

**ZUCCHINI SQUASH**

1 baby zucchini, about 5 inches long, 1¼ inches in diameter
sour cream
fresh garden thyme

Cut zucchini in thin slices. Do not peel. Spread zucchini slices with sour cream and sprinkle each slice with a pinch of fresh chopped thyme leaves.

Serves 8.

## KOHLRABI

¼ cup sour cream
1 teaspoon olive oil
1 teaspoon finely chopped savory leaves
salt
2 kohlrabi

Mix sour cream, olive oil, savory and salt to taste in dip bowl. Peel and cube kohlrabi, and serve on toothpicks on plate around dip bowl.

Serves 8.

## CARROTS

2 carrots
½ teaspoon prepared mustard
½ teaspoon olive oil
1 teaspoon fresh, chopped mint leaves
4 tablespoons sour cream
paprika

Halve the carrots crosswise and French them. Arrange carrots on plate around dip bowl. Mix mustard, olive oil, mint, and sour cream together, and serve in dip bowl. Just before serving, sprinkle dip with paprika, to color.

Serves 8.

## GREEN PEPPERS

1 bell or frying pepper
1 tablespoon sour cream
1 teaspoon chili sauce
½ teaspoon fresh, chopped mint leaves
dash of salt

Remove stem end, pith, and seeds from pepper and slice in strips about ¼ inch wide.

Mix other ingredients in dip bowl and arrange pepper strips on plate around the bowl.

Serves 6.

## CUCUMBER

1 small cucumber, an inch or less in diameter
3 slices wheat bread
sour cream
1 sprig fresh dill

Slice unpeeled cucumber very thin. Cut bread in circles, same size as cucumber slices. Spread bread circles with sour cream, top with cucumber slices, and sprinkle lightly with freshly chopped dill leaves.

Serves 4.

## A FRESH GARDEN PLATTER

Red Plum tomatoes
Yellow Pear tomatoes
scallions

radishes
salt
fresh, chopped basil leaves
olive oil

Halve the Plum tomatoes. Leave the yellow tomatoes whole. Cut about half the green tops off the scallions, and strip off any outside dry leaves, and outer skin of bulbs. Cut green off radishes, and slice each five times, part way through the root end, to make a flower effect.

Mix coarse salt and basil in dip bowl. Roll the vegetables lightly in olive oil, just enough so that salt will adhere. Arrange this colorful selection on a pretty platter around the dish of basil salt.

## FISH DIPS

Use fresh herbs, sour cream, and horse-radish, and you will come up with some palate-tickling fish snacks.

## SHRIMP DIP

A quickie.

1 pound green shrimp
1 teaspoon finely chopped dill leaves
1 teaspoon tarragon vinegar
horse-radish (prepared)
chili sauce

Boil shrimp with fresh dill and tarragon vinegar, as per **Shrimps No. 1, in Sauce.**

Remove shells and devein, and stick a toothpick in each shrimp.

Mix dip in a small dish, half horse-radish and half chili sauce. Place shrimp on plate around the dip dish.

## PICKLED HERRING

2 8-ounce jars Vita Party Snack Herring in Wine Sauce
ringed onions from herring jars
2 teaspoons onion juice
1 cup sour cream
1 teaspoon chopped summer-savory leaves

Drain and discard liquid in herring jars. Cut herring in about 1-inch squares. Arrange on plate around sauce cup. Mix onions, onion juice, and sour cream together with the savory. Chill in the refrigerator.

Serve herring bits on toothpicks, and the dip in a sauce cup.

Serves 16.

## SMOKED SALMON

¼ pound thinly sliced, smoked salmon
2 tablespoons sour cream
1 teaspoon fresh chopped dill
1 clove shallot, minced
paprika

Cut salmon into about 1½-inch lengths. Roll and spear each roll with a toothpick.

Mix sour cream, dill, and shallot in sauce dish, and sprinkle with paprika. Serve salmon rolls around the dip.

Serves 16.

## SMELTS AU VIN BLANC

Very special, for fish lovers.

- 2 pounds smelts
- ¼ cup flour
- 1 egg
- salt and pepper
- ¼ cup bread crumbs
- ¼ pound butter
- 4 sprigs fennel, each sprig about 7 inches long
- ⅓ cup tarragon vinegar
- ½ cup white wine
- juice of half a lemon
- ⅓ cup peeled, minced shallots

Split the smelts down bellies and clean. Let any roe remain. Cut off all fins.

Roll the smelts in flour. Beat the egg and dip the smelts in the egg. Sprinkle the smelts with salt and pepper and bread crumbs, and brown them in hot butter in a skillet, turning frequently. Remove from pan and let the smelts cool.

When cool, split the fish part way down the backs and pull out backbones. Lay fennel on the bottom of a deep casserole, arrange the smelts on the fennel, then pour on vinegar with wine and lemon juice and add the shallots. Let marinate at least 24 hours in the refrigerator.

## TWO CHEESE "DOS"

### Cheddar-Cheese Canapé

A quickie.

⅛ pound Longhorn Cheddar, cut very thin
pumpernickel or rye bread
½ teaspoon prepared mustard
½ teaspoon finely cut-up chives
1 teaspoon catchup

Cut cheese and bread in 1-inch squares. Mix mustard, chives, and catchup and spread on bread. Top each piece of bread with a square of cheese. This canapé may be served cold, or heated in the oven.

Serves 6.

### Spiced-Cheese Canapé

This takes time and quick handling.

olive oil
white bread
¼ pound sharp Cheddar cheese
3 teaspoons butter
½ cup milk
1 tablespoon soya sauce
1 teaspoon powdered ginger
¼ teaspoon caraway seeds
1 teaspoon anise seeds
1 teaspoon finely chopped sweet-cicely leaves
salt and pepper
3 tablespoons ale

Line a standard-size roasting pan with heavy aluminum cooking foil and brush the foil lightly with olive oil. Cut enough circles of bread to cover bottom of roasting pan. Shave cheese. Melt butter in skillet on top of stove, and add milk and cheese, stirring constantly. When cheese starts to melt, add soya sauce, ginger, caraway and anise seeds, and sweet cicely. Sprinkle lightly with salt and pepper.

When the mixture starts to boil, add the ale and continue to stir rapidly. When sauce thickens and is smooth, remove from stove and cool for a minute. Dip one side of bread in cheese; place dry side down on foil in roasting pan. If there is any left-over cheese, spoon it onto the center of the canapés.

Set pan in oven under broiler, and when cheese starts to bubble, remove from under broiler and keep in warm oven. This canapé can be made several hours ahead of time and re-heated.

## TWO GOOD EGGS

### Curried Eggs

18 hard-boiled pullet eggs
1 teaspoon curry
4 tablespoons sour cream
1 tablespoon olive oil
½ teaspoon salt
¼ teaspoon pepper
capers

Remove eggs from hot water and shell them immediately under the cold-water tap. Cut in halves, remove yolks, and place in a bowl. Mix yolks with all the other ingredients except the capers. Stuff the egg whites with the curried yolks and arrange on a platter. Dot each half with four capers.

**Savory Eggs**

6 hard-boiled pullet eggs
2 slices lean bacon
2 tablespoons olive oil
1 teaspoon fresh, chopped savory leaves
1 teaspoon mustard flour (dry mustard)
salt and pepper
paprika

Shell eggs as in preceding recipe. Slice in halves and place yolks in a bowl. Broil the bacon till crisp. Remove from pan, let drain on paper towels, and then chop very fine in a wooden chopping bowl.

Mash the egg yolks with the olive oil until creamy. Add bacon, savory, mustard, and salt and pepper to taste. Spoon yolks back into egg whites and sprinkle with paprika.

This recipe makes fine stuffed eggs for picnics, for which use large eggs and, proportionately, more seasoning.

## MUSHROOM-STEM CANAPÉ PIQUANT

A delightful way to use up extra mushroom stems.

4 cups mushroom stems (or small mushrooms)
⅓ cup thinly sliced shallots
¼ pound butter
1 pinch cayenne pepper
1 teaspoon ground ginger
1 teaspoon chopped lovage leaves
1 teaspoon chopped thyme leaves
1½ teaspoons salt
½ teaspoon black pepper
¼ teaspoon sugar

2½ teaspoons flour
½ cup light cream
¾ cup heavy sour cream
½ cup sherry
1 tablespoon soya sauce

Slice mushrooms crosswise in thin slices. Sauté mushrooms and shallots in butter in an iron skillet, stirring constantly. When shallots are transparent, add the spices and herbs, salt and pepper. Cook the mixture until lightly browned, stirring continuously.

Now dip mushrooms and shallots with a perforated spoon into a bowl. Leave juice in skillet. Blend sugar and flour into the juice, and cook until quite brown, but do not burn. This means stirring rapidly. Add the fresh and sour cream and cook until sauce begins to thicken.

Return mushrooms and shallots to skillet and bring to a boil. Fold in sherry and soya sauce. Remove from stove, chill, and freeze. When ready to serve, thaw, heat thoroughly, and serve in pastry canapé shells.

## COCKTAIL SAUSAGES AU VIN ROUGE

1 4-ounce can Vienna sausage
butter
½ cup zinfandel wine
½ teaspoon mustard flour (dry mustard)
¼ teaspoon finely chopped sweet marjoram leaves
½ teaspoon finely chopped thyme leaves

Sauté sausage in buttered skillet, shaking pan constantly. When the sausages begin to brown, add wine, mustard, and herbs, and cook until most of the wine is absorbed. Serve on toothpicks.

## TURKEY ROSMARINUS (ROSEMARY)

For a bit of leftover turkey—

pumpernickel bread
butter
fresh, minced rosemary leaves
leftover turkey
stuffed olives

Cut bread in 1-inch-size squares, butter, and sprinkle with a pinch of rosemary. Slice leftover turkey very thin, and cut to fit on bread. Top each turkey canapé with a thin slice of olive.

## SOUPS DU JOUR

See the **flavor chart** for herbs best to use with soups.

Soups deserve more attention than they have had since the decline of domestic help in households. The modern housewife, thinking in terms of reduced dishwashing, serves many one-dish meals. Some soups, such as bouillabaisse, fill the bill for this kind of meal. Others are mere appetizers.

We start with two of the latter, well worth the extra dishwashing and the time for preparation. They are both herb soups.

## PARSLEY SOUP

1 small boiled potato
¼ cup fresh, minced parsley leaves
1 teaspoon flour
¼ teaspoon salt
⅛ teaspoon pepper
2 cups light cream
1 tablespoon butter

Peel and mash the potato. Mix in the parsley, flour, salt, and pepper, and blend with the cream. Add butter, and bring to the boiling point on the stove. Serve immediately.

Serves 3.

## SOUPE A L'OSEILLE (SORREL)

This recipe was given us by a French countess. There are many variations, but this is the basic French way of making it.

2 cups French sorrel leaves
2½ tablespoons butter
¾ teaspoon salt
6 cups chicken stock
pepper
2 egg yolks
toast

Wash sorrel but do not dry. Chop leaves, then wilt them in a deep iron skillet over low heat on the top of the stove. Add butter, let melt, then add salt and stock, and sprinkle lightly with pepper. Let come to a boil. Simmer for about 10 minutes. Beat egg yolks, mix with a little hot stock, and remove the skillet from the fire. Then stir egg yolks into soup. Do not boil after eggs are added.

Place a toasted slice of bread in each soup plate, and add soup.

Serves 6.

## BEET CONSOMMÉ

Another appetizer soup.

- 2 cups beet juice
- ½ teaspoon chopped lovage leaves
- ½ teaspoon chopped thyme leaves
- 2 beef bouillon cubes
- 2 tablespoons sherry

Boil beet juice, herbs, and bouillon cubes until cubes dissolve. Add sherry.

Serves 3.

*When coal and wood were the only fuels used in the kitchen range, the cook kept the fire burning all day long, not for cooking alone, but, in winter, to heat the kitchen, and, even in summer, to heat water for the household; for a hot-water boiler was generally attached to the range. There was always a pot simmering on the stove, and ever-good, ever-hot stock was ever ready for making soups and gravies.*

*Now that everybody is cooking with gas or electricity,* pot-au-feu *is but a pleasant memory. The modern cook makes her stock and keeps it handy, in the freezer. Here is a two-in-one recipe for making stock, and, at the same time, boiled beef.*

## BEEF STOCK

- 1 knucklebone, fat and meat removed, about 4½ pounds
- 1 marrowbone
- 3 pounds shin of beef, bone in
- 10 shallots, peeled

2 teaspoons salt
1½ teaspoons pepper
*bouquet garni:* 2 sprigs thyme, 1 sprig sweet marjoram or origanum, small handful parsley sprigs

Have butcher saw knucklebone and marrowbone, each into four parts. Place shin of beef, knucklebone, marrowbone and shallots, salt, and pepper in cocotte. Cover with water and set on high fire. When water comes to a boil, reduce heat and let simmer. Skim off foam, as necessary. Cover the cocotte and continue to simmer, 2–3 hours, or until meat comes easily from the shinbone. During the last ½ hour, add *bouquet garni* and more salt if necessary.

Remove beef and set aside to serve hot, or cold, with horse-radish sauce. Let bones simmer in stock about another hour. Discard bones, *bouquet garni,* and shallots, and strain stock through a sieve. Chill. When cold, the fat will rise to the top, and the stock will jell to the consistency of aspic. Skim off the fat, and reserve for future use. Keep stock in refrigerator or freezer.

Makes about 5½ pints stock.

Following are two soup recipes which call for **Beef Stock.**

## BEEF CONSOMMÉ

A soup for a cold winter's day.

4 cups **Beef Stock**
2 tablespoons soya sauce
1 teaspoon ground lovage seeds
½ teaspoon finely chopped thyme leaves
2 tablespoons sherry

Bring to a boil all ingredients except sherry, and boil for 10 minutes. Strain, add sherry, and serve.

Serves 6.

## HERB MADRILÈNE

The soup for a hot summer's day.

5½ pints **Beef Stock**
*bouquet garni:* 1 sprig lovage, 2 sprigs sweet marjoram or origanum, 2 sprigs thyme, 6 sprigs parsley
5½ envelopes Knox's unflavored gelatin
½ cup sherry
3 lemons
fresh, chopped parsley

Set aside 1 cup cold meat stock. Add *bouquet garni* to remainder of stock, bring to a boil, and let boil for about 5 minutes. Discard *bouquet garni.*

Mix gelatin in cold stock, add sherry, and mix all together with hot stock. Pour into a bowl and chill.

Just before serving, break up madrilène with an electric mixer. Serve with a wedge of lemon and a sprinkle of fresh chopped parsley to garnish each cup.

Serves 18.

*The following soups are hearty.*

## BORSCH

This traditional Russian soup is a blood soup, but today it is most often made with beet juice, substituted for the blood.

1 quart meat stock
1 pound cooked, chopped beets, with juice
1½ cups chopped red cabbage
1 onion, chopped fine
1 pinch finely chopped thyme leaves
½ teaspoon anise seeds
2 crushed cloves
salt and pepper
sour cream

Mix together all the ingredients except the sour cream. Boil until tender. Strain or not, as desired. Russian borsch is usually served heavy, but some prefer to mash it through a sieve. When soup is served, add 1 tablespoon sour cream to each serving and let it float on top. Do not stir cream in.

Serves 10.

## BOUILLABAISSE

A one-dish meal chowder.

1 pound green shrimp
2 teaspoons salt
2 teaspoons finely chopped dill leaves
2 teaspoons finely chopped parsley leaves
¼ teaspoon finely chopped thyme leaves
1 potato, peeled and diced
1 large carrot, cubed
⅓ cup ringed onions
½ teaspoon black peppercorns
few grains cayenne pepper
1 bay leaf
¼ cup halved shallots
1 clove garlic, minced
½ green pepper, cut in thin strips
3 tablespoons olive oil
1 pound scallops
1 pound fillet of flounder, cut in 1-inch pieces
1 pound fillet of cod, cut in 1-inch pieces
1 cup cut-up tomatoes
⅓ cup Rhine wine
4 tablespoons light cream

Boil shrimp in water to cover, with 1 teaspoon salt and the herbs, for about 10 minutes. Remove shrimp, shell and devein, and cut crosswise. Strain stock into a cocotte, add potato and carrot, and simmer.

Meanwhile sauté onions, shallots, garlic, and green pepper in olive oil in a skillet. When onions are transparent, transfer ingredients from the skillet to the cocotte. Add peppercorns, cayenne, and bay leaf. As soon as the carrot and the potato are parboiled, add the shrimp, the scallops, and all the fish, the tomatoes, the wine, and more water if necessary. This is a thick chowder and should not have too much liquid.

Cover cocotte and let simmer for 20 minutes. Blend in cream.

Count on 1 cup to 1½ cups for each serving, depending upon whether your guests have been sitting in the office or have just blown in off the ski slopes.

Makes 10 cups.

Serve with **shallot bread**; for dessert, *café noir* and a green herb salad.

## LEFTOVER GARDEN SOUP

A peppery, frosty-weather, one-dish luncheon soup.

This is to vegetable cookery what bouillabaisse is to fish cookery. A little of just about everything goes into it. For this is the soup to make right before the first hard frost. Garner the last few of this and that.

½ pound ground beef
¼ teaspoon finely chopped thyme leaves
¼ teaspoon finely chopped sweet-marjoram leaves
½ teaspoon finely chopped lovage leaves
salt
1 medium potato, peeled and cubed
1 medium carrot, cubed

½ cup sliced okra
⅓ cup Lima beans
1 cup cut-up snap beans
1 medium-sized tomato, cut in pieces
4 shallots, peeled and cut up
1½ cups finely chopped red cabbage
16 peppercorns
2 beef cubes
4½ cups **Beef Stock** (or water)

Mix meat and the chopped herbs, sprinkle with salt to taste, and make meat into small dumplings about ¾ inch in diameter.

Boil vegetables in stock or water with beef cubes and peppercorns. Just before the vegetables are done, add the meat dumplings and boil another 10 minutes.

Serve in deep soup plates with buttered sesame wafers heated in the oven.

Serves 8.

*In our house, dinner generally ends with plain fruit or cheese and crackers for dessert, and coffee. But when we have guests to dine with us, we like to do something special. Most of our favorite desserts have fruit for the main ingredient.*

*The main ingredient in the following continental dessert soup is the fruit of roses.*

## ROSE ALMOND SOUP

3 cups fresh rose hips (fruit of roses), measured after removing seeds
4½ ounces blanched almonds
½ teaspoon salt
dash of pepper

5 tablespoons sugar
4 drops vanilla extract
2 tablespoons flour
1 cup red wine
cognac
whipped cream

The apple rose (*Rosa pomifera*) bears large, handsome, ornamental hips, and they are among the best to use for this soup because of their size. Fruits of the *rugosa* are also large. During the Second World War the English gathered even the little haws (English for hips) of the hedge rose to make soup and jam because the fruit of roses was reported to have a higher Vitamin C content than oranges, which were so scarce and so high priced in wartime England that they were practically unobtainable.

Some gourmet shops carry dried powdered rose hips, and if you use the dried, measure two thirds of the amount called for with the fresh.

Pick the fresh hips after the fruit has turned a bright orange-red. To prepare, cut off blossom and stem ends, slice in halves, and spoon out the seeds. Wash hands immediately to prevent tiny prickers on the hips from working into the skin. Put the hips and the almonds through the meat grinder, finest grind, and then turn hips and almonds into a saucepan. Add salt, pepper, sugar, 5 cups water, and vanilla. Stir in flour and bring to a boil. Boil for 5 minutes, stirring constantly. Add wine and boil 5 minutes more, continuing to stir. Chill.

Serve cold in glass dessert dishes. Just before bringing to the table, spoon a teaspoon of brandy onto each serving and add a dab of whipped cream.

Serves 16.

Another of our favorite fruit desserts with a continental flavor is:

## PEAR FLAMBÉE

3 Bosc pears
lemon rind
1½ tablespoons sugar
½ teaspoon finely chopped rosemary leaves
butter
½ cup Rhine wine
3 tablespoons brandy

Halve pears, cut off blossom and stem ends, and spoon out the seeds. Do not peel. Line a casserole with a piece of heavy aluminum cooking foil, fold foil over edge of casserole, and set pears on foil. Grate a little lemon rind over the pears, sprinkle with the sugar and the rosemary, and dot with butter. Pour wine into foil in casserole, not on the pears. Cook in a preheated, 300° oven until pears are done, but not soft.

Then place pears under the broiler until the sugar starts browning. Spoon the brandy into the seed cavities in the pears, light brandy with a match, and burn about half a minute.

Serves 6.

## CHAMPAGNE COMPOTE

Light and delectable.

1 bunch white grapes
1 bunch red grapes
5 cups cubed pineapple, with juice from the can
8 ounces chopped candied ginger
1½ teaspoons chopped spearmint leaves
2½ pounds frozen raspberries
1⅔ cups champagne

Halve grapes and remove seeds. Mix grapes and pineapple in a bowl and add ginger and mint. About an hour before serving, add the frozen raspberries. Just before bringing to the table, add the champagne.

Serves 16.

## ANGEL FRAPPÉ

A rich dessert.

1 pint cream
1 1-pound can lingonberries or common cranberries
4 teaspoons minced mint leaves
1 dozen macaroons
cognac

Whip the cream until stiff. Stir in the lingonberries and the mint leaves. Then crumble the macaroons and fold them in.

Serve in small glass dessert dishes. Just before bringing to the table, spoon a small hole in the center of each serving and fill with a teaspoon of cognac.

Serves 16.

## A DESSERT FRUIT SALAD

10 lettuce leaves
1 1-pound can pineapple (10 slices)
3 avocados
10 teaspoons sauterne
1 teaspoon finely chopped rosemary leaves
sour cream
sugar
cinnamon

Arrange a leaf of lettuce on each dessert dish and add a ring of pineapple. Peel, remove seed, and cut avocados into thin strips, and arrange around pineapple. Sprinkle a teaspoon of wine and a pinch of rosemary on each salad. Top each with a teaspoon of sour cream. Lightly dust with sugar and cinnamon.

Serves 10.

**DESSERT PANCAKES**

2 eggs
½ tablespoon white flour
½ teaspoon baking powder
1 tablespoon sugar
1½ tablespoons light cream
⅛ teaspoon salt
1 slice bacon
confectioner's sugar

This recipe calls for a special Scandinavian pancake pan which is divided into seven small circles.

Mix all ingredients except the bacon and the sugar in a bowl. Heat pancake pan, grease with the fatty side of the bacon, and drop 1 tablespoon batter in each circle. When the little pancakes bubble and start to dry on top, turn them with a spatula. Grease pan for each batch. Sprinkle pancakes with confectioner's sugar.

Serves 4.

Serve with **lingonberries,** or cranberries.

*A plate of candied mint leaves and borage flowers makes a tasty bite to pass with after-dinner coffee and brandy.*

## CANDIED MINT LEAVES AND BORAGE FLOWERS

mint leaves
borage flowers
2 egg whites
granulated sugar

Pick a handful of perfect mint leaves and wash and dry them on paper towels. Pick a handful of borage flowers in full bloom.

Beat the white of the eggs, dip the leaves and flowers into the egg white until coated, and then sprinkle with sugar. Spread out on a sheet of wax paper to dry in a cool place.

## MINT BRANDIED PEACHES

To keep.

2¼ pounds sugar
4 teaspoons finely chopped fresh spearmint
3 quarts peaches
2 cups brandy

Sterilize 6 self-sealing Mason jars and caps in a deep pot of boiling water.

To make sugar syrup, mix sugar, 3 cups water, and mint in a saucepan and let come to a boil. Boil 10 minutes.

Meanwhile set another pot of water on to boil. Dip peaches in the boiling water, then in cool water, and peel. Cut in halves and remove pits.

When you have a pint of peaches, cook them in the boiling sugar syrup for about 5 minutes. Remove with a slotted spoon, drain for a second, then pack in a hot sterilized jar.

After you have cooked all the peaches, boil the remaining syrup until it thickens, adding more sugar if the syrup is too thin. You should have about 2 cups of sugar syrup. It is difficult to give exact measurements because some peaches are more juicy than others.

Cool the syrup, add brandy, bring to the boiling point, fill jars with syrup, and seal.

Makes 6 pints.

# 10. BEFORE WINTER COMES

It is late summer, and by now a goodly stack of polyethylene bags of fresh herbs for the winter season are in the freezer. These and your own home-frozen vegetables taste wonderfully refreshing during a spell of dour winter weather. One advantage of having a home garden is that you can pick the produce absolutely fresh, and freeze it before it has had time to lose vitamins by lying in vegetable bins. The less time between picking and freezing, the better the frozen product. So hurry and fill the freezer containers with surplus crookneck squash, with snap and Lima beans, with kohlrabi and okra, and, unless you have a root cellar, carrots, beets and winter squash, and the extra rutabagas. Peppers freeze well too. If you did not gobble up all the sugary-sweet mange-tout peas as soon as they formed pods on the vines, the peas went into the freezer early in the season.

## FREEZER PROCESSING TABLE—VEGETABLES IN THE VEGETABLE AND HERB GARDEN

| *Vegetable* | *Time of Harvest* | *Preparation* | *Blanching Time* |
|---|---|---|---|
| beans, Lima | young, | shell, wash | 60 seconds |
| | mature | | 2 minutes |
| beans, snap | mature | cut or French | 3 minutes |
| beets | small | whole | 2½ minutes |
| carrots | young, | whole | 4½ minutes |
| | mature | French | 2 minutes |
| chard greens | young, fresh leaves | wash | 2 minutes |
| kohlrabi | young | peel, slice | 60 seconds |
| okra | young | whole | 3 minutes |
| mange-tout peas | young pods | whole | 60 seconds |
| peppers | mature green, not red | slice | do not blanch |
| rutabaga | mature | peel, dice | 60 seconds |
| squash, crookneck | young | cube | 3½ minutes |
| squash, winter | ripe | *see next page* | |
| tomatoes | ripe | make juice *see below* | |

### TOMATOES

Select ripe fruit. Cut in small pieces, but do not peel. Cook in a saucepan until soft enough for most of the pulp to pass through a sieve. Mash pulp in sieve. Add 1 teaspoon salt, ⅛ teaspoon pepper, and 1 teaspoon fresh chopped basil leaves to each pint of juice. Bring to the boiling point, chill in ice water, and freeze in Ball glass freezer jars. These are special, and not the kind used for canning.

### WINTER SQUASH

To prepare winter squash for freezing, peel, cube, and cook until quite soft. Then mash and cool. Package and freeze.

To freeze the other vegetables in the table, assemble:

6-quart (or larger) pot with cover
6-quart (or larger) pot without cover
strainer big enough to hold a pound of vegetables
freezer containers
ice cubes

Wash and prepare the vegetables. Bring water in the covered pot to a rolling boil. Place no more than 1 pound of vegetables in the strainer. Immerse the strainer with the vegetables in the boiling water. Start timing when water resumes boiling.

Fill the second pot with cold water and ice cubes. When the vegetables are blanched, immerse the strainer in the ice water. Keep adding ice cubes to the cold-water pot, to assure quick cooling. Drain most of the water off the vegetables, package in standard freezer containers, and freeze immediately.

To freeze vegetables in the freezer compartment of a refrigerator which has a temperature down to at least 10 degrees Fahrenheit, freeze only small amounts, no more than 3 pounds at a time, and place the containers directly on the metal surface of the compartment. Do not let them touch each other.

If you rent a locker in a freezer plant, take your prepared vegetables to the plant directly after blanching and chilling. If you have your own home freezer, just follow the directions that come with the appliance.

## BACK INTO THE GARDEN

The vegetables continue to ripen, and many of the herbs are going to seed. Pick the seeds of coriander before they fall to the ground and store them whole in a bottle. Gather the ripe seeds of lovage. The seeds of lovage have very oily meat, and therefore dry them in the oven on low heat, then put them through the meat grinder, finest grind, and store in a tightly closed jar in a dry place, for use in soups.

Harvest shallots after the tops brown. Dig them on a sunny day and spread out the bulbs on a stone terrace or on a board in full sun. If there is a sign of approaching rain, take the shallots in at nightfall and spread them out again the next clear day. When the outer skin feels dry, shake off earth from the bulbs, pack in old string onion bags, and hang in a cool place in the cellar.

## LIGHT FROST PREDICTED

When the weather bureau forecasts the first light frost in your area, get out the old Army blankets, draperies, tarpaulins, or what-have-you, and at nightfall, cover the tender plants. In the Vegetable and Herb Garden this means the tomatoes, the pineapple sage, okra, squash, dill, basil, fennel, and the beans, whose leaves shrivel at the very mention of the word "frost."

Cover the peppers also, for although a light frost may touch only the upper pepper leaves, the plants will not continue to bear fruit if thus blighted.

The other herbs and vegetables will come through and continue to grow if still in their prime.

In the Garden Salad Bowl, cover the cucumber trellises, the tomatoes, the peppers, the basil, and the dill; in the Annex, the pineapple sage.

After a day or two of this first cold snap, summer temperatures usually again prevail, and you may then enjoy a reprieve—a week or ten days—often longer—of growing weather.

At this time the late plantings of lettuce and radishes take hold. Salad burnet, chives, and parsley continue usable. Upland cress and rocket still lend a tangy flavor to green salads. The borage will be hoary. The leaves, tough and too hairy to eat, will be touched by the frost, but the flowers continue to come until a real freeze blackens the whole plant. Costmary and sorrel continue good.

Except for the triumphant delight a gardener experiences when he hoodwinks the fall season of a week or two of time, harvest of the fruits of plants susceptible to light frost might as well begin when the first frost threatens. So if you prefer, skip the old-blanket-and-tarpaulin routine and react to the weatherman's forecast of the end of balmy summer nights by trundling out the wheelbarrow to the garden and loading it up with ripe squash and the other late harvest produce.

If you have a cool storage room, where the temperature does not drop below the freezing point, pick only the ripe tomatoes, then cut the tomato vines with the green fruit still attached and hang the vines on pegs in the room. Green tomatoes ripen very well this way. Otherwise line out the unripe fruit on a sunny window sill.

Store the hydrator in the refrigerator full of cucumbers, peppers, fennel, and kohlrabi.

The root crops—carrots, beets, and rutabagas—and the cabbage may remain in the garden until after a hard frost.

Of the gleanings, a handful or two of beans, etc., make **Leftover Garden Soup.**

Then sit down and consider what's best to do with the perennial herb plants in the Vegetable and Herb Garden, the Garden Salad Bowl, and the Annex.

## IN AND OUT WITH ROSEMARY

The pineapple sage which grows both in the Vegetable and Herb Garden and the Annex must be brought indoors. It is a tropical plant and cannot stand cold. Cut it back, because at the end of summer it will be leggy, and if it is root-bound, cut away any dead roots, repot in fresh potting soil, and winter it as a house plant.

The sweet marjoram in the Vegetable and Herb Garden will stand considerable cold weather but will not live through our zero and below-zero winters. Pot it, if you will, for kitchen use, but not to hold it over. It is too easy to start again next season from seed.

The biggest decision to make is the one concerning the rosemary. Rosemary is classed as a tender plant, but we have been told that it lives through winter on Cape Cod and in parts of Long Island and New Jersey. So try it. You may have a warm pocket in your locality. We have tried and tried on our herb farm. We have risked our biggest and strongest plants in all sorts of places. We have tried north, south, east, and western exposures; we have set plants against a wall; we have mulched deep. Hoping to find a hardy strain for propagation purposes, we have succeeded only in losing some of our handsomest rosemary, for every plant we have risked in the ground for the winter has been as dead as the dodo bird, come spring. So we say to people who live in hills like the hills of New England, pot your small plants in the fall and set the pots in a cold frame. Rosemary is so nearly hardy, it will come through zero spells nicely, under the cold-frame glass. Lacking a cold frame, a pit or regular greenhouse, you have no choice but to lug all your rosemary plants into the house before winter comes.

As for the other perennial herbs in the three gardens, unless you want to pot a selection to winter on the kitchen window sill—in which case, see Chapter 4, **On the Terrace and the Window Shelf**—just "leave them be," at least until the spring.

## AFTER A HARD FROST

Harvest the root crops and the red cabbage.

Cut off the blackened stems of the following herbaceous perennials, the ones which die down to the roots and sprout anew in the spring: lovage, tarragon, mint, costmary, sweet cicely, chives, and French sorrel. Compost this refuse along with tomato and cucumber vines and the frosted residue of the other annual plants—the borage, the dill, the basil, etc.

*But* let lemon balm go through the winter with its leaves on, and do not prune the woody plants, the sage or hyssop or the garden thyme till spring.

After the ground has frozen, cover the carpeting thyme which grows in the cracks between the bricks in the Vegetable and Herb Garden and the Garden Salad Bowl, and around the sundial in the Annex, with a springy mulch. Short-cut lengths of hemlock boughs are very good for this. Throw an armful, also, over the crowns of the tarragon, and over the mint bed.

For herbs such as sage and hyssop and thyme, simply see that the mulch you used in the summer garden is snugged up around the plants like a muffler, leaving the tops exposed to sun and air.

## FOR THE TERRACE GARDENER

Those handsome terra rosa ring pots which you have enjoyed all summer long on the terrace cannot be left out in winter. Clay pots usually crack in freezing weather. Wooden tubs and planter boxes withstand cold weather better and may come through with no more harm than the weathering of the paint, but the plants in exposed containers will not survive in cold climates.

It is possible to sink the wooden planter boxes and tubs in the garden, with the tops level with the surface of the soil, and mulch them after freezing weather, but this is a bit rough on the boxes and tubs. It is better to bring wooden containers as well as clay pots indoors, and winter them in a conservatory, in a regular or pit greenhouse, or in a cool cellar.

You may keep rosemary, and almost any number of other kinds of herbs, in containers in the cellar from the first freeze to April showertime, provided there is a room walled off from the furnace, or that the cellar does not house the furnace. It happens that our heater is on the ground floor and our cellar is cool and damp. Here potted rosemary stays delightfully fresh and green all winter long. So does the *Myrtus communis,* the true myrtle.

Some of the other herbs—for example, lemon verbena and pineapple sage—go into a more or less dormant state. They drop their leaves, but they sprout cheerily when put out in the sun again the following spring. It is unnecessary to water the plants, unless the soil gets dry.

Potted plants in a permanent terrace box should be treated like any other potted plants—that is, taken in. Hardy herbs planted directly in soil, as in the kitchen terrace box, may remain in the box over winter. Those listed for our kitchen terrace box—the tarragon, the garden thyme, the mint, the winter savory, the garden sage, the origanum, and the chives—should winter over, even in a very cold climate, if mulched. When a heavy frost comes, bank the box well with hemlock boughs or a similar mulch, and when the ground freezes, throw an armful of the boughs over the top of the box.

Pot and take in the rosemary in the kitchen terrace box, of course, early in the fall.

## LOOKING FORWARD

We hope that you have a bountiful summer. We hope that the salads grow green and lush in the outdoor salad bowl, that the vegetables are both decorative and delectable, and that the sweet herbs are so aromatic with essential oils that you will want to do it all over again next year, the same way. If this is the case, the perennial herbs left in place in the garden over the winter may grow right there where they are, and as they are, for another summer or even two or three more seasons, if you wish—with the exception of mint.

When the ground thaws in the spring, first look at the mulch and see if it will do another summer. If it is salt-marsh hay, it will, for salt hay does not rot for at least three or four years. If you have used a Michigan type of peat, it may have rotted sufficiently in one season to make good humus—in which case, dig it into the ground and get new mulch. If the mulch is still usable, rake it off the rows where the annual vegetable, lettuce, and herb plants are to be seeded again, and fertilize. Pull back the hay around the perennials far enough to feed them. Toss the hemlock boughs off the paths, and from around the sundial in the salad bowl; let sun and air reach the little creeping thyme, which should be as green in the spring as it was in the fall when you covered it. Take the boughs off the tarragon and the mint.

Then, when the ground dries out enough to be worked, dig up that great spreader, mint. During the summer of 1959 we watered the round mint bed in the Vegetable and Herb Garden, and the smaller square bed in the Garden Salad Bowl, with **Liquid Manure.** The plants grew lusciously. The following spring we took a look at the roots. The whole bed in the vegetable-herb garden, 4 feet in diameter, planted with four small plants the previous spring, had in one season become massed with mint stolons. They were packed so tightly together, they were literally strangling each other. The entire circle had become as completely "pot-bound" as any mint ever raised in an actual pot, for the metal strip had acted exactly like the sides of a pot. The same thing had happened to the mint in the salad bowl. The answer to this is that any mint which is confined in a small bed must be root divided in the spring of the second season to make a thrifty growth. For root division of mint, see **Pot-Bound** in Chapter 4.

In the open garden, costmary is also a lusty grower, but when confined, it persists and keeps growing well, in spite of crowded conditions. You can generally leave costmary in a small bed for three years without hurting the plant. Then root divide.

The tarragon will thrive in one spot for four years, perhaps even five, after which it should be taken up in the spring—for this is the best time to propagate herbs by root division. Pull the roots apart. Tarragon roots come apart very easily, and you will note that the center roots are woody, and they may be rotting, for in this way nature lets the plant divide itself. New plants spring from the new side roots. Chances are, however, that wire worms or other worms have been working their way into the dead center roots. So cut off any dead or rotting roots and burn them. Then replant only the vigorous new growth, in a *new* location, as crop rotation is a wise practice to follow for the perennial herbs listed in this book. Move them at the time of root division to a new place in the garden, and they will sprout with renewed vigor. At the same time rotate the annual crops, the lettuce and the root vegetables, the tomatoes and the cucumbers, the sweet marjoram and the fennel and the others.

Perennial herbs also to be propagated by root division are:

garden sage, hyssop, winter savory, garden and carpeting thyme, origanum, French sorrel, lemon balm, and chives.

To divide woody-stemmed plants such as sage and hyssop, use a sharp knife. Cut away the main hard core, then replant only young stems with a good root growth attached.

The following herbs in the three gardens are easily propagated from cuttings: rosemary (will root quickly if just stuck in a glass of water), pineapple and garden sage, and hyssop.

Sweet cicely, lovage, and salad burnet self-sow.

Cuttings may of course be taken in the fall of the year, if you have a suitable place to propagate in winter. Otherwise, all this is winter armchair talk.

## A GARDENER'S NIGHTCAP

The garden has been put to bed, the salt-marsh hay, the hemlock boughs, or what-have-you, are mulching the plants in the frozen ground, and snow, that natural mulch, is, we hope, lying in an easy drift over the cold frames and blanketing the earth. Tubs and pots are in the greenhouse or cellar and a planter box of herb plants sits on the kitchen window shelf.

Now comes the time to open the new year's bright seed catalogues, and to reflect on last year's successes and failures. Now is the time to evaluate your crops, to consider how well, or how adversely, certain kinds of vegetables, salad plants, and herbs did in your kind of soil.

As a solace for failures and a toast to future success, we offer the following recipe which you may serve by the open fire while talking shop with your gardening friends.

**GLÖG – A WINE FLAMBÉE**

6 cardamom seeds (buy these at the drugstore)
1 gallon tawny port wine
1 quart pale dry cocktail sherry
1 tablespoon cloves
1 tablespoon anise seeds
1 teaspoon powdered ginger
1 cup seeded raisins
6 large pitted prunes
5 cinnamon sticks
1 sprig rosemary (for remembrance)
1 small lump sugar
1 cup brandy

Remove shells from cardamom seeds. Combine all ingredients except the lump of sugar and 1 teaspoon brandy in a stainless-steel bowl.

Place bowl on an alcohol stove or an electric hot plate. Put sugar lump and the remaining teaspoon of brandy in a stainless-steel tablespoon, and light the brandy with a match. As soon as the sugar caramelizes, add it to the wine.

When the glög begins to warm, stir the ingredients and light the wine with a match. As the flickering tongues of blue flame lick around the bowl, stir, stir. When finally the flaming wine is hot, dip the liquid only, not the raisins and other solid ingredients, into cups, and serve immediately.

Invite twelve to sixteen herb-minded friends to toast with this glowing drink the prospects of the sleeping garden awaiting the spring sunshine and showers and your eager administrations.

# INDEX